SOUL GROWTH ISSUES
SOUL GRIEF CHOICES

Published By:
Parah Publications

ISBN 0-9723861-0-6

Fred Rawlins
www.fredrawlins.com

Cover art and design by Gary Bennett
Black Canyon City, Arizona

Printed by United Graphics, Illinois

BY
FRED
RAWLINS

SOUL GROWTH ISSUES
SOUL GRIEF CHOICES

CONTENTS

SPECIAL ACKNOWLEDGEMENTS

I feel the people who have come into my life and helped me in so many ways are the true creators of this work. My best friend Armando DeLeon has been helpful beyond measure in getting the business side of my work organized and professional. This has taken so much pressure off of me, giving me the time to spend on the creative portion. Armando's banking background keeps things on the business front running smoothly.

Arlene, Lou, and many other special friends have given me the encouragement to complete this work when I was feeling exasperated with life. The list is endless in terms of people who have had a part in this project. I have indeed had many angels in my pathway.

Two of my very good friends who initially flew me out to Arizona, Sal and Carol Grande, have been such an inspiration in my life. Truly angels in my path.

Beth and Bill, KEZ 99.9 FM radio personalities, have been more than supportive of my work on their show for the past 11-plus years. Truly angels in my path.

Lastly I want to mention my gratitude to Vicky Hay, Ph.D., for her tremendous aptitude in editing my book. Incredible as it may have seemed to me at first, she was able to take my work and make it better. You cannot imagine the reluctance writers have when someone else critiques their work. I did not know an editor could make something better. I thought they just wanted to display their knowledge and make one look foolish. (I still think some of them do.) But, how fortunate for me I found someone who has the ability to transform something ordinary perhaps into something extraordinary perhaps.   *—Fred Rawlins*

Achildhood bereft of its innocence, a life of turmoil, anguish and heart aches all typify Fred Rawlins' life story. These experiences have of course helped to shape Fred's philosophy about life and the many adversities that we may all encounter during our Soul Development while on the earth plane. Through adversity, Fred gained strength; through sorrow, Fred developed empathy. Through Prayer and Meditation, the Spirit has made known to Fred incredible insights concerning a Souls journey while attempting to return to God in perfect love, which he so powerfully shares in this book

In this writing Fred shares many of these insights with staggering simplicity as well as providing a step-by-step approach for achieving our own Spirituality! The parallel that Fred's book draws between organized religion and Spirituality is done with such intellectual capacity and clarity that you find yourself rethinking all that you have been taught.

When you first read that our Soul chooses our parents, our gender and our race as well as many of the experiences (we call them challenges) we encounter in each life, during the Review Before Return Process, it is consciously mind-boggling. However, as you read on you begin to grasp how the proposition of such a plan tends to be extraordinarily more Divine and therefore far more enhancing in our effort of Soul Development.

Fred helps you realize that we are indeed part of that Divine Spark and *without a doubt* worthy of God's Love!

Fred's philosophy leaves the reader with the recognition that if a belief is truly of God it can never divide the population by race, creed or color, nor will it take away Freewill. Such wisdom prompts an indescribable, awesome awakening of the Soul.

The metaphysical messages and insights about life contained within the pages of this book are a must-read for anyone who feels set adrift by life's turmoils.

Governor of Arizona, 1987–1991

I n the summer of 1987, the chapters for this book began to appear in a vision I had during my daily meditation. The information was given in such rapid succession, I had no time to think about what I was writing. Hurriedly I began to write down the information, although I knew it would mean that I would be late for an appointment. However, I felt I must continue to write down what I was being given. There was no time for thinking, just writing!

Later that same day, after I returned home from my errands, I was eager to reread what I had received in the vision during my morning meditation. At the time I was given the chapters for this book, I assumed I was to write about what I perceived to be relevant to these chapter titles from a conscious perspective. I was wrong. I did not realize that it would take me fourteen years to complete this writing.

I had no way of knowing at the time that it would take me that long to experience (and therefore understand) a portion of the book and to achieve forgiveness in relation to some of the contents.

Visions as well as psychic phenomena were not new to me. I have been giving psychic readings since I was nineteen. But for eight years previous to the vision for this book, I was not involved in the psychic realm at all.

In the staid accounting offices where I spent many years working as controller and secretary/treasurer for large manufacturing companies, I hesitated to let my psychic side be known.

It was approximately a year or so before the vision for this book that I began to have more and more frequent visitations from the Spirit Realm. From an early age, I have always been aware of having three "angels" around me. During the time I was focused on my accounting career, I sensed their presence but had very little input from them. Then one night I was awakened by the shaking of my bed. I sat up and saw my three angels at the foot of the bed. They conveyed (communication with the Spiritual Realm is a conveyance of thought energy, not verbalized words) to me that I must go back into psychic work.

Noteworthy: Angels, Spirits, guides, etc. will reveal themselves to you visually, in keeping with certain criteria. For example, some of the Angels that have been given charge over us for our protection have never been in human form. Visitations from these entities would take on a more ethereal or otherworldly form. However, when Spirits who have made the transition from the physical to the Spiritual Realm appear to a loved one who is still on the earth plane, they will always be recognized as they were known while human form. As an example, if you had a child who died while you were still alive, a visitation from the child's Spirit would always be recognized as your child. However, if you as well as the child were deceased, in the Spirit Realm you would recognize each other as familiar Spirits, not as parent and child.

Each encounter we have with Spirits, Angels, guides, etc. while in human form can be linked to a previous incarnation we had. For example, if an individual whom we do not know in the current life repeatedly appears in our dreams or visions, that Spirit most certainly has a prior life connection with us. Many times our Angels or Guides are individuals we have been around in a past incarnation, perhaps casually or perhaps intimately.

In one of my own previous incarnations, I was with Edgar Cayce when he was Ra Ta, the Spiritual Leader of Egypt. In that particular life I served as one of his "lieutenants." There were seventeen of us at the time. One particular vivid remembrance of this life is of Ra Ta giving information out to the masses who had gathered to hear him in the courtyards of the pyramids. In my vision of this event, I saw Ra Ta standing atop a platform. That platform was supported by what we would think of now as scaffolding. The moonlight played brilliantly off the sides of the pyramids. They seemed to reflect the moonlight out onto the masses who had gathered. When I mentioned to a present-day friend of mine about how shiny the sides of the pyramids were, he told me they were in fact covered with marble at the time Napoleon discovered them. I did not know.

The role the seventeen "lieutenants" played was to go among the people in the crowd and help them to interpret and understand the information that Ra Ta was sharing. I have been told that these seventeen Souls will reappear just before great changes begin to occur in the world to help usher in the new understanding. Each of the seventeen will write, speak and give insight that will enhance the transition, which will result in many years of peace.

We can also attract Spirits who are tricksters and very negative. These attractions can occur when we are stressed, angry, bitter or sick; or in any combination of the aforementioned. They can also occur when a person who is not Spiritually balanced dabbles with the Ouji Board, holds séances, or does automatic writing. After the 9/11 incident, many negative Spirits were set loose on the world because of the tremendous outpouring of fear. When we perceive a Spirit in our midst, we should always say: "If you come in the name of God, you are welcome. If not, you must go into the Light." When this statement is made, the Spirit *must* comply!

When my three Angels begin to convey the need for me to return to my Spiritual work, I felt annoyed. I felt I was being asked to give up the security of my accounting profession to work in an area that was uncertain and certainly not widely accepted. Therefore, I was determined to do nothing more as a psychic. I had worked very hard to get to the top in my profession as an accountant and was not ready to give that up. With that thought I went back to sleep

A few weeks passed without incident. Then one day while I was doing some gardening in my back yard, I felt a hand on my left shoulder. I was startled. The gate to my back yard was always locked, and no one was at home but me. Before I could turn around to see who was there, a resounding thought filled my mind and echoed throughout my entire being. "You must go back into your psychic work."

Before I could think, I stood up and said out loud, "Get off my ass. Find someone else—just leave me alone!" As I turned around to go into the house, I saw my 83-year-old neighbor standing by the fence staring at me with her mouth open and shaking her head back and forth. Later that evening, she called to inquire if I was all right.

Yet, as is quite often the case with the universe, circumstances had already been set in motion that would change my life drastically. At the time these events occurred, I was living in Texas. When the oil economy went bust, the company that I worked for filed bankruptcy. A year or so later, it went out of business. Although I tried valiantly to find another job, sending out 703 résumés, I could not.

At last circumstances led me to reconsider my previous refusal to work in the psychic field. I am so glad that the Spirit is wiser than the conscious mind. I am so thankful that God does not turn away from those who think they know where they are going and what they are doing. I am very humbled to do the work that I do today. Our efforts to help one another are really all that we leave behind when we depart from this planet.

It is my hope as well as my prayer that this book will provide for many the bridge between Religion and Spirituality.

■ "Experience": All that we encounter in our lives, commonly called challenges.

■ Bi-liable: Having an impact on two people involved in an experience, not just one.

■ Chakra: One of the seven energy centers identified with points on the human body.

■ Challenge (experience): This can be a person, event or circumstance usually connected to Past Lives and karma.

■ Freewill: The vehicle with which we accomplish Soul Development.

■ Inner Being: Our Soul Mind. We access our Inner Being through Meditation.

■ Karma: The reward or punishment for acts done in present or previous lives. Positive as well as negative; decisions that are made emotionally rather than Spiritually, represent our Soul Growth Issues for current and subsequent lives. Talents for music, art, finance and so on represent knowledge acquired and used successfully in Past Lives.

■ Life Expression: A current incarnation.

■ Meditation: Listening to God. Closing down our five senses so that our Soul Mind (part of the God-force) can connect with us in human form.

■ Miracles:

● Partnered Miracle: These are the events that transpire in our lives where some other person(s) participated. These events are representative of the Faith of every one involved.

● Solo Miracle: These events occur exclusively of our own Faith. Our belief system attracted the event into our lives. Like begets like!

Past Lives Record: A complete record of all that our Soul has been; this record represents every word, every thought and every deed that we have expressed. This record is timeless and can represent eons.

■ Prayer: Talking to God. This is our conscious supplication, usually based on wants, needs and desires.

■ Reservoir of Knowledge: An area where information that pertains to our Soul Development is stored. Our Past Lives Record, our Soul Mind, our Chakras, and our pineal gland are all characteristic of such Reservoirs.

■ Review Before Return Process: A process in which a soul about to return to the earthly plane reviews its Past Lives Record and makes certain decisions about its pending reincarnation. Because of this process, our Past Lives Record is key to the current Life Expression. Our Soul will choose parents, gender, and race that will provide the stage on which our Soul Development can be played out. This Review will also denote astrological influences that are applicable to the current Life Expression.

■ Soul Development: This is accomplished through the Soul Growth Issues as well as Soul Grief Choices that we encounter with each life. Soul Development is determined by response; Spiritual or emotional in relationship to each issue.

■ Soul Grief: Challenges (experiences) that the Soul has chosen to have in the current Life Expression, void of karma.

■ Soul Grief Choice: These choices are made during The Review Before Return Process for the sole purpose of God's love being made manifest on the earth plane.

■ Soul Growth: The development of the Soul in response to life challenges (experiences).

■ Soul Growth Issue: A challenge (experience) chosen by our Soul during The Review Before Return Process.

■ Soul Mind: Part of the God Force that must be accessed through Meditation.

■ Soul-Self Responsibility: Taking responsibility for one's Soul Development by giving thanks for each challenge (experience) encountered during the earth sojourn.

■ Soul-to-Soul Resuscitation: This happens with the individuals which we meet in each Life Expression.

■ Spiritual Contract: The arrangement made during The Review Before Return Process for certain challenges (experiences) with each Life Expression. Our response to these challenges (experiences) determines our advancement.

■ Value: Each challenge (experience) has a value that can be assessed by using one or more of the following criteria:
- Emotional
- Financial
- Mental

Once a value has been assessed we must stop and ask ourselves if we are willing to trade our future for such a paltry sum.

1

YOUR "HEALING COW"
THE MIRACLE OF SPIRITUALITY

The first memory I can recall from my early childhood is of two cows, horns locked in battle, in the lane in front of our house. This incident harks back to the time when I was about two years old. That visual image was immutably embedded in my memory, even at such a young age.

I would learn as my life progressed that I would have many experiences, some symbolic, some not, where cows would play an important role during the process of my Spiritual development. Over the years cows have appeared repeatedly in my dreams. Dreams usually contain the components, people, events and things of our life experience that convey a message of Spiritual significance to us. And cows as such have had a profound impact on the development of my Spiritual psyche.

As I grew up, my family lived in many different environments. Primarily we were associated with the earth and farm animals through the work that my father did to support us. From the time I was born until the 1950s, we lived for the most part on dairy farms. Then my dad purchased a regular farm. We grew crops like corn, watermelons, and okra. We also had hogs, cows, chickens, horses, and mules.

During the early '50s, my dad drove a dump truck and a logging truck part-time. He hauled fill dirt for various people, as well as cutting and hauling pulpwood. While driving dump trucks, my dad was run over and had his neck and back broken. The doctors said he would never walk again. However, he did. From this accident, my dad received enough money to put a large down payment on the farm he bought.

My dad could not read or write. Growing up he always had to work to help support his family. Both of my parents' families were mostly farmers. School was not so important in those days. My dad also had a real problem with drinking. He was pretty much a drunk during the '40s, '50s and early '60s. During that time, he also struggled with another issue: womanizing.

Consequently, after he bought the farm, he deposited me, my sister, my two brothers, and my mother there. Weeks would pass and we would have no idea where he was. He expected my mother, me, and my sister to keep things going. My two brothers were too young to help at all. Needless to say, with my dad's focus on drink and women, eventually we lost the farm. After that, my dad worked again on dairy farms for a while, and then he spent many years as a sharecropper.

I remember accompanying my dad when I was around twelve years old to work on a dairy farm. I overheard him tell a coworker about a cow that had "gotten down and could not get up." I recall my dad saying that the cow would have to be put out of her misery. This of course meant that the cow would have to be destroyed. At the time and on any farm, the accepted method of putting an animal out of its misery was to shoot the animal between the eyes. Knowing that this would happen upset me tremendously.

I ran out of the barn and found the cow lying down in a special holding pen that was used for sick animals under the care of the veterinarian. I knelt down by the cow and asked God to restore her to health. "Please, God, allow this cow to get up, and make her well," I implored. At first there was no response, so again I beseeched God, while placing my hands on her head, to please heal this cow.

My mother had always told us that God expected us to be kind to dumb animals. Remembering this, I felt that the only thing I could possibly do in this circumstance was to offer up a prayer for the cow. I could not think of anything else that I, at my inexperienced age, could possibly do.

Within a very short time the cow stood on her feet, walked to the nearest feeding trough and begin to eat. I prayed and it worked! I have never forgotten this Miracle.

There was never a doubt in my mind that God would respond with a Miracle (Healing). I had asked for the cow to be restored to health and *expected* that to occur.

You see, it had only been a few months before that our mother had been bedridden and gravely ill that another Miracle had occurred. All the neighbors thought mother would surely die. She had not eaten for several days and was showing no signs of improvement. My dad would go off each day to work on the dairy farm and leave my sister, since she was the oldest, in charge of me and my two brothers.

One day after my dad had been gone to work for a few hours; there was a knock on the front door. When my sister opened the door, there stood a woman dressed all in white, with the most beautiful red hair I have ever seen. Her hair seemed to glow, it was so bright. She quietly said that she had come to help our mother. She went straight into mother's room, although she had never been to our home before. My sister, my two brothers, and I followed and watched as this woman caressed our mother's head, speaking in a whisper to her all the while. After what seemed to be a very brief time, the woman stood up and walked toward the front door. As she reached the front door she turned and said, "Your mother will be fine now." As quietly as she came, she walked out the front door. We never saw her again.

As we were turning around to go back into our mother's room, she came walking out and said she needed to prepare supper. People who lived on farms always called the evening meal supper and the noon meal dinner. And they still do to this day. Our mother began to prepare the evening meal, at the same time scurrying around picking things up, while she continually fussed at my sister and me because she thought the house was such a mess. It was if she had never been sick! Mother always said, "We may be poor, but we do not have to be dirty!" She was back!

THE FAITH OF A CHILD

So, when the incident with the cow happened, you might say that I possessed "blind faith" or "childlike faith." The fact of the matter is that I prayed and expected results! I just knew that God would respond with a miracle. God had healed my mother a few weeks previously, hadn't He? Why would He not heal this cow?

It is imperative during our sojourn here on this planet that we not forget that we have been admonished by various Spiritual teachings to have this same kind of child-like faith and expectancy in our daily lives.

We become so caught up in our efforts of day-to-day living that we forget how simply miraculous life really can be. As such we become "conditionally afraid" to ask for and to expect Miracles (Healing).

THINKING ABOUT MIRACLES

Taking time to reflect on those circumstances that we have experienced as miraculous, helps to shore up our faith-building efforts for the future.

Spiritually, it is fundamental for our Soul Growth that we think on previous episodes of Miracles (Healing) often, so that we may be sustained in times of subsequent challenges (experiences).For a guide, see Appendix Two.

While it may be true that the conscious mind is inherently capable of having only one thought at any given point in time, it is also true that we have Freewill. With this Freewill we can choose to saturate our thoughts with Miracle (Healing) thinking, each day, THIS day, of our lives. Taking time to re-read the Miracle (Healing) Journal you have prepared is helpful. Reading your Journal aloud to friends or family can be inspirational as well.

Many times, because of extenuating circumstances beyond our control (conscious), we allow ourselves to become bogged down with fear and doubt. It is during these times that we convince ourselves that a Miracle (Healing) cannot occur. In essence we kill our healing cow by saying and thinking that there is no hope. Allowing ourselves to become immersed in the energy of the struggles that are occurring in our lives at the time, we sentence our healing cow to death.

MIRACLE THINKING

It is not a difficult process. But how would YOU define a Miracle? I like to think that Miracles are a Healing!

Do you need a Healing (Miracle) in your relationship, finance, job, thinking, speaking, actions, living environment, or health? Where would you focus the energy of Healing (Miracles)? With your Freewill approach you have the power to decide! It begins with your thoughts, your words and your deeds (the actions you take).

However, our need for or want of a Miracle (Healing) will not bring God's response. It is our faith! Childlike faith! Faith Expressed Above Rationale! Belief that everything will work out for the best, even though we may not know (consciously) the how (details). That is Faith! The how is the rationale.

Each of us needs to run through the barnyards of our minds, find our Healing Cow (the event that denotes your Miracle) and recapture the childlike Faith of expectancy for Miracles (Healing) in your daily life. Miracle (Healing) thinking begins as we, by our own Freewill, saturate our thoughts with Miracle (Healing) remembrances. Thinking about Miracles (Healing) leads to speaking about Miracles (Healing), and accordingly taking action to invite the Miracle (Healing) into our lives.

The human psyche, left to its own devices, becomes habituated to sameness. Freewill is the spark that ignites the Power of our Thoughts, our Words, and our Deeds to bring about change. This Power can redefine unsavory behavior patterns that we imprinted on earlier in our life. One of the most colossal by-products of redefining habituated behavior patterns is the gift of being able to co-create our future along with God each day. Freewill also imposes an accountability for our Soul Growth.

Reminders (conscious) are good! If you want things to be different, your Freewill is the means of access to your Power. Freewill implies SELF! Freewill begins with Self making a decision (thoughts) that certain changes (deeds) are necessary. Talking (words) to those who will be immediately affected by these changes is worthwhile. Finally, take steps (deeds) to set up reminders in the home or work environment that will trigger the conscious mind to anticipate change.

Example: Let's say you want a new job. Your (thoughts) have been leaning in that direction for awhile.

You have had conversations (words) with various family

and friends about this. And, you have posted your resume on an Internet job site (deed). OK? Now what? How can you further prepare the energy for job change?

Set up your living and work environment to provide you with "reminders" that you are expecting change! Why? Because, until now you have been habituated on sameness. Leaving a drawer or a door a third of the way open in every room of your home will serve as a "reminder" (consciously). Each time you notice it, you will be reminded that you do not want sameness. You are expecting change! You are empowering your thoughts! Leave Post-Its in each room, reminding yourself that change is under way. Your Freewill approach has ignited the power of your thoughts, words and deeds to accomplish this change!

Before you start leaving doors and drawers open around the home, you should make one last effort in preparing your environment. It will help to tell the other people in your household what the "reminders" are for. When sameness is brought to task, it will evoke the attention of others in your immediate environment. Senility set aside, providing others with the knowledge (power) of your new approach can have more than one benefit! Doors and drawers left open are REMINDERS! Simple as that. Reminders, simply put, are the changes (conscious) we make that serves to invite Miracles (Healing) into our lives.

TWO KINDS OF MIRACLES

There are two types of Miracles (Healing):
1. Solo Miracles (Healing)
2. Partnered Miracles (Healing).

A Solo Miracle (Healing) takes place as a result of our conscious efforts. Our prayers. Our prayer and meditation efforts. Our Faith. Faith (Belief) Expressed Above Rationale. The Miracle (Healing) occurs in our health, finance, relationship, in any facet of our life, as a result of "our" (conscious) efforts.

A Partnered Miracle (Healing) is accomplished as a direct result of someone else's intervention. A person who prayed with you. The individual who gave you the winning lottery ticket. Or the doctor who assisted you in conquering the medical malady that threatened your life.

Solo as well as Partnered Miracles (Healing) are activated by Faith! Belief that the change will occur even though we don't have the answer or know-how. Solo Miracles honor your Faith. Partnered Miracles (Healing) honor the provider's as well as the recipient's Faith.

THE FAITH THAT BRINGS MIRACLES

We must come before our God asking, with the Faith (belief) of a small child, for the Miracles (Healing) that are available to us in the day-to-day experiences of our mortal (body, mind and Spirit) sojourn.

Although mortal in our experience, we are also Spiritual! Our Faith (belief) prompts our Spirit (Soul Mind or God Self) to supply the Miracle (Healing) we need. Faith releases the ability of our God Self! Our Soul (Spirit, Soul Mind, God Self) is part of the God Force. We ARE individualized Gods in a mortal existence. When we remember this, Miracles (Healing) can occur!

In our childhood, we are more aware of the connection with our Spirit (Soul Mind or God Self) than in our adult lives.

As we approach our adulthood, this awareness begins to fade. The conscious mind, chronologically speaking it seems, is easily distracted at an early age. Quite often as children, we are far more cognizant of our Higher Selves than we allow ourselves to be in adulthood. During our pursuit of life, liberty, and happiness many of us are enticed to take a detour.

This indulgence often is the consequence of our frenzied search for fulfillment.

Other detours can also inhibit our Spiritual progress. In my work I have often observed individuals avoiding anything that evokes a connection with God. This has usually been due to the demanding, and many times distasteful, environments of religious dogma to which they were subjected in their formative years. Little wonder that the fear, guilt, and control approach has soured many from all that bespeaks a Spiritual connection for their lives.

We tend to get swept away by the energy that recreates! This distraction, as mentioned earlier, occurs by our exposure to various dogmas, parents, peers, academia and so on. We are "customized" into individuals whom we often do not like. Consequently, in our adult life—usually not until our forties, though—we set about the process of redefining ourselves.

What power, to realize that we possess the ability to recreate ourselves by way of our Freewill! Power of any sort can cause us to become heady (conscious-minded) and lose sight of our intended course in our life. Simply put, we were created to be Companions and Co-Creators with God. Apart from making us Companions and Co-Creators with God, our Freewill can ignite the Power of our Thoughts, Words and Deeds to accomplish, during our human sojourn, just about anything we want.

Organized dogma often imposes so much fear, guilt, and control onto an individual's life that the connection with the Inner Spirit (Soul Mind, God Self) is lost. The sum and substance of our Spiritual Growth simply means we care about others.

SPIRITUALITY IN ACTION

Not long ago, a client shared a remarkable story that speaks volumes about how we treat one another. One day a homeless man came into her office and asked if she would be kind enough to help him write a letter to his daughter.

He wanted to let his daughter know he was doing well and to tell her not to worry, for he would be in touch in the near future. My client's boss was out of town that day so she felt she could spare the time to type the letter for the man. The homeless man told the lady after she typed the letter that he did not have a lot, but would like to give her a dollar for her kindness. She refused, telling the man that the company she worked for paid her very well and he need not worry about payment.

The next day the homeless man returned and insisted that the woman take the dollar for her efforts. The woman's boss, having returned from his trip, overheard the conversation and told her she should accept the dollar as it was a matter of pride for the homeless man.

Reluctantly the woman took the dollar. After work she stopped at the grocery store to buy a few items she needed. She also decided to buy a lottery ticket with the dollar the homeless man had given her. A few days later to her amazement she found out she had won a multi-million dollar lottery! She tried on many occasions, without success, to locate the homeless man. She wanted to share the good fortune with him.

Was that her reward for helping a homeless person without regard to what she would receive in return? Was this an angel in her path, allowing her to express her Spirituality (caring about others) unselfishly? You decide.

Spirituality should make one rejoice, not despair! If we are to have Spiritual Healing in our lives, we must first have a Healing in the way we respond and interact with others. We should never be so pompous as to think that everyone should embrace the same beliefs that we hold as truth.

Without regard to race, creed, color or religious belief, we must remember: Spirituality is how we treat one another. All else is theory. We should approach God in a childlike manner, believing and asking that our Faith be renewed. It is our Faith that will bring God's response, not our needs, wants, or desires.

2

TWENTY-TWENTY BLINDSIGHT

In choosing to inhabit our present life, we are in essence continuing a journey that our Soul embarked upon many former lives ago. Diverse in experience as well as indoctrination, this journey can leave us scratching our heads as to how our Souls will ultimately reconnect with God. It is from this position the discussion of Soul Growth Issues begins.

Continually living in the past is one of the most recurrent, counterproductive ways in which we continue to use our conscious minds. It is as though we have forgotten to look within, making our own effort to connect with our inner portion (our Inner Spirit or Soul) of the God force. I believe this is due largely in part to the various dogmas that exist today. Many religious tenets teach the existence of an all-loving God, yet continue to embrace the sentiment (judgment) that no Soul can know God without the acceptance of the religious sect's ideologies.

We have been conditioned to believe that meditation (going within, connecting with our Inner Spirit) is inauspicious, therefore unnecessary, in our efforts to know God. Yet, it is only through prayer and meditation that we become true companions of God.

How incredible that we have allowed others to persuade us that we should disregard the one place that God truly exists (within us; our very Souls). How incredible that we have been taught that FREEWILL is not in our best interest. Yet our Freewill choices provide the most direct and immediate impact that we can have on our Soul Growth Development, while we are in human form.

WHAT IS FREEWILL?

Freewill choice is "the stuff" with which karma is made. Freewill choice is also the vehicle that transports our lives into the future. Freewill choice is the key ingredient for independence as well as individuality.

Through some model of organized dogma, most of us have been taught and have come to believe that God allows Freewill. Yet many would try to convince the population as a whole that our lives are predestined. In line with that thinking, many espouse the philosophy that our trials and tribulations here on earth are God's plan for our lives.

If that were true, then why would God allow us Freewill? It is in fact our plan (our Past Lives Record), for the most part, that brings the perceived adversity into our lives.

However, individuals can experience some circumstances (via their Soul Mind choice) solely for the purpose of being the instrument of God's Love displayed. These are what I refer to as "Soul Grief Choices." (See Chapter 3).

As an example, think of the occasion when the Christ figure spit on the ground and made mud and put it on the blind man's eyes. The Gospel of John reports that Christ's disciples asked Him, "Who sinned, this man or his parents that he was born blind?" Jesus answered by saying, "Neither. . .but that my Father's works may be made manifest through this man" (John 9, 1-3).

It is my belief that this man, during his Review Before Return Process, chose to re-enter the earth blind.

His lack of eyesight would become a current life experience (challenge) until the healing miracle of sight was wrought in his adulthood. His blindness was not inflicted upon him as punishment, nor for the meeting of karma, as is usually the case with the Past Lives Record subject matter.

Being born blind in and of itself would ordinarily speak to Past Lives. We know this person did not experience blindness as karmic, according to his Past Lives Record. ("Neither. . .but that my Father's works may be made manifest through this man").

I believe this man chose blindness (a "Soul Grief Choice") so that he could be the instrument that God would use for the onlookers to build their faith when the miracle of sight took place.

OUR "LOST" KNOWLEDGE

We have become a civilization of people who have been conditioned to forget our inner connection with a Higher Power. We must awaken to the knowledge that we are indeed Companions and Co-Creators with God. I often recall Edgar Cayce's insight regarding the ancient civilization of Egypt, which thrived at the time the pyramids were built. He said the people who built the pyramids were more in tune with their Creator than we are today.

What happened that the knowledge of such an advanced civilization has been lost? I cannot help but believe that the more we turn away from God and embrace the physical, the less we know (consciously).

Conditioning over the years to forget our connection with our Inner Spirit has left us without the benefit (help) of the all-knowing force (our Inner Spirit) that we all possess. Our Inner Spirit (Soul Mind) is all-wise!

Our conscious mind is limited to what we have learned or been taught in any given life. We have willingly allowed the archetypes of our parents, friends, coworkers and academics to become attached to our lives. At the same time we continue to complain about the varied discomforts our acceptance of such beliefs have caused for us.

This conditioning, for the most part, occurs in our formative or childhood years. Incidentally, it is in the childhood or formative years of our lives that the Soul Growth Issues of the greatest magnitude to our current lives will be experienced. After all, it is in the formative or childhood years that we are totally dependent on another human being.

HOW OUR PAST LIVES MOLD OUR PRESENT LIFE

It is in this state the Soul is confronted with our Past Lives record (remembrances). The childhood or formative years are karmicly influenced via, if you will, a Silver Cord connected to our Past Lives Record (remembrance).

This record (remembrance) is the energy that defines the vibration for our experience in the current and subsequent lives. What we have sown, we will reap. If we have abused, denied or harmed another Soul in any way, the formative or childhood years are the stage on which our Soul Mind will arrange the "characters" from our Past Lives with which we are to interact in the present life.

Our Soul Mind (our Past Lives Record) determines the parentage and therefore the race that each life will have, as well as the gender and its initial indoctrination. All of these elements are keyed to our need for Soul Growth with each life. As such, it is important that we comprehend that experiences we may encounter, although difficult, have been programmed to our current life. This has occurred by way of our Past Lives Record, which reflects our Soul Growth Issues.

In other words, we have pre-selected certain experiences (for our Soul Growth) prior to our return to this planet. So, you might ask, how can that which our Soul Mind (Spirit) designates necessary for our Soul Growth be so difficult? The dilemma comes of course in our futile attempt to rationalize the Soul Growth Issues selected in what I refer to as "The Review Before Return Process," (or RBR process) with our logical, conscious minds.

I believe there are two occasions in which our lives pass before us in their entirety: The Near-Death Experience, which everyone has heard about, and the experience I have called "The Review Before Return Process" (or RBR Process). I believe it is in the Review Before Return Process that our Soul Mind determines the availability of experiences which have the potential to facilitate our Soul Growth. These experiences, Soul Growth Issues, are extrapolated from our Past Lives Record.

CHALLENGES AND THE GROWTH OF OUR SOULS

These Soul Growth Issues are usually the experiences (challenges) we encounter while in human form, which we must endure without the ability to adjust them, consciously, in any way.

We can however, Spiritualize the experience (Soul Growth Issue) by giving thanks for each one as it is encountered in our lives. Conventionally, it may sound somewhat foolhardy to give thanks for the experiences of our past; however, we must, if we hope to succeed in our efforts of Spiritual Growth.

While in human form, unless we learn to meditate, we are limited in the insight that we can receive from the Spiritual realm. Insight from the Spirit Realm can only occur through our five senses, in a three-dimensional form. Our Spirit cannot use the five senses to communicate as long as they are in external or conscious use. For that reason meditation is a must if we want our Spirit to provide us with insight.

Many of our experiences (Soul Growth Issues) can be understood only through a Spiritual approach (giving thanks for the experience), in that our Soul Mind (via our Past Lives Record) chose the experience before our return to this planet. These are our Soul Growth Issues.

Throughout this writing I will remind you that we do in fact have the power to attract the future we want. It is staggering when you stop to understand how much of our lives and therefore our power is lost by continually focusing on the past. Thoughts (energy) are things. Spoken words set into motion an energy that resonates through the Universe. Our actions are usually the combined force of the thought energy as well as the word energy.

I should have, I could have, you should have, you could have, we should have, we could have. . . . Circumstances would have been different if. . . .all TWENTY-TWENTY BLIND-SIGHT! How many times have you heard someone say, "If I knew then what I know now? . . ." How many times have YOU personally used the phrase, if this would occur, or, if that had not happened? Having your head so far up an IF serves no purpose except to obscure the future.

If you are like many people who have not learned to stop reflecting on the past except to give thanks for it, learn from it, and move forward, then you, too, have been caught up in this perpetual loop of Twenty-twenty Blindsight.

UNDERSTANDING SOUL GROWTH ISSUES

Various reasons as well as excuses (you choose the label) can be proffered for our inclination to continually visit the past. First and foremost the human psyche seems to be thrown for a loop when we encounter an opposition or a change in the pattern of energy around our lives.

Panic sets in when our job, our home, or our relationships are brought to a place of change. *Fear of the unknown.* Such fear is characteristic of a conscious-based approach.

This onset of fear speaks volumes about living totally in the conscious realm. **Reminder:** Our conscious minds are limited to what we have learned or been taught in any given life. Our Soul Minds are unlimited, containing a record of our Past Lives and our Present Life, as well as unlimited insight pertaining to our future.

Whether they think the challenge was of their own making or not, many people will immediately assume what I like to call the "Spiritual Fetal Position." In other words, they pose their energy in a position of whining, moaning and groaning.

It matters not that we may be king, queen or pauper; everyone will encounter challenges (experiences) during a human life expression. Challenge boundaries by race, creed, color, belief or station in life do not exist.

Circumstances (experiences) that test (conscious thought pattern) our lives will continue to occur with each life expression. Change however, brings newness: new people and new experiences. Assorted challenge (experience) components are necessary for our growth, consciously as well as Spiritually.

CHOICES: CONSCIOUS OR NOT

When confronted by any adversity, it can be very helpful to first qualify the adversity. In other words, analyze the adversity to determine the origin.

Did your Freewill choices of this life cause the dilemma? Or was the adversity at hand not of your making—consciously (this life), that is?

Whether you think the adversity is by your own choice consciously (this life) or not, you should try and determine if you have the resolve for the adversity at hand. If so, apply the resolution, give thanks for the experience and move forward into your future.

On the other hand, when you analyze the adversity and you do not consciously have the resolution, you must remind yourself that what you are dealing with is a Soul Growth Issue or a Soul Grief Choice.

Chosen by your Soul Mind in light of your Past Lives Record, the adversity represents a spotlight on a Soul Imbalance. You have the opportunity to re-address the Soul Imbalance in the current life expression, and, hopefully, to heal it. The Soul Imbalance is presented in the current life expression for the single purpose of rebalancing your Soul.

We are not expected to have the answers consciously for those adversities chosen by our Soul Minds (via our Past Lives Record) during our Review Before Return Process. Once we have qualified the adversity and determined that it is from our Past Lives Record, we must give thanks for the experience, ask for wisdom to learn and grow from it, and move forward into our future.

When we give thanks for the adversity from our Past Lives Record, it is absorbed into our Spirit (Soul Mind). The Soul Mind is where the true meaning is found as it pertains to this life. This meaning will be "time-released" into our consciousness as needed, or as we are capable (ready) to understand.

HOW NEGATIVE ENERGY
CAN TAKE OVER OUR LIVES

If we whine, moan and groan about the adversity, we add to the negative energy (conscious thought pattern) that already exists, and we lay the foundation for a similar adversity to occur again and again in the future. Perhaps it will happen with a different face, in a different place, but until we respond Spiritually, the same old song and dance will play over and over again.

REMINDER: "Our future rests on the foundation of our thoughts, our words and our deeds." Consequently it is the responsibility of each one of us to keep our pathway (conscious minds) clear. Additionally, what we perceive (consciously) as the negative adversity (chosen in our Review Before Return Process) can in fact be a blessing, presented as a Soul Growth Issue.

Negative thinking serves to envelop our lives, cutting us off from our Soul Minds, while destroying little by little our ability to move forward. In essence we become Spiritual Zombies, cut off from any input of our Soul Mind.

The Spiritual destruction precipitated as a direct result of over-evaluating the past can be rectified by establishing a sincere desire, along with an honest effort on our part, to move forward. This cannot be a now-and-then attempt made with a ho-hum approach. We must continually be watchful (conscious) not to allow negative thoughts sanctuary.

CONTROLLING NEGATIVE ENERGY
BY CONTROLLING OUR THOUGHTS

Keep in mind as you start this process, you have been conditioned for the greater part of your life to respond to the input generated by the conscious mind only. Such conditioning quite often has been negative (fear-based).

Signs of this are thinking the worst first and continually looking through the pain of disappointment (past) toward the future.

Many people will express their desire for a meaningful relationship while remaining afraid of being hurt again. Their fear is sameness. It is vitally important to our Soul Growth that we remind ourselves continually that what we fear, we attract!

The conscious mind is limited to what it has learned or been taught in any given life. Sameness is a conscious, past-related fear. This can be changed, however. Just realize that it takes the same amount of effort (energy) to hold onto a fear as it does to focus on a desire. If it is true that we attract what we fear, why not shift that energy to the desires we have for our lives? Then we may say, in faith, what we DESIRE we attract!

We cannot stop the birds from flying over our heads; however, we do not have to allow them to build nests in our hair! So it is with negative thoughts. We do not have to give them sanctuary!

We have Freewill! We must continually monitor our thoughts, clearing away the negative thought (energy) and replacing it with a positive thought (energy).

The use of positive affirmations—such as "God renew my faith and help my unbelief," "God have mercy," "God's Love reigns supreme in my life"—or speaking or thinking positive words like *love, joy, peace,* and *happiness* will replace the negative thought, helping us to accomplish the balance that is so crucial to our Soul Growth Issues.

The first step in changing our lives is changing our thoughts. Our life will chase after our thoughts, but our thoughts will not chase us down the street.

I have been saying for years on radio and television that life can be better than our thoughts, but WE have to change them first!

DEALING WITH LIFE'S CHALLENGES

Challenges (experiences) of some type will always be part of the human sojourn. However, it is not the challenges (experiences) that will determine our Soul Growth. It is our response to the challenge (experience) that will triumph over our Soul Growth Issues. Giving thanks is fundamental in our pursuit of Soul Growth. In fact, it is the key to cultivating our Spiritual balance for this and subsequent lives.

While it is true we may have to endure the experience, it is also true that by giving thanks (Spiritualizing the experience) we will not have to repeat it over and over again. And, most important, when we spiritualize it, the challenge (experience) will not consume us emotionally.

What a Spiritual revelation to understand that each person and each challenge (experience) we encounter has been brought into our lives with our agreement (during the Review Before Return Process) before we returned to this planet. All of this for but one single purpose, confronting our Soul Growth Issues.

EXPERIENCES WE CAN CHANGE

During my nearly thirty years of counseling with people I have come to realize that we can change, do away with, avoid or alter some of life's challenges (experiences). These are the challenges (experiences) that our Freewill (conscious) choices have established in our current, present life sojourn.

Usually it is our emotions that have precipitated such challenges (experiences). And we must remember that using emotions to make decisions offends our Spirit (Soul Mind) in human form. This knowledge is primary in our effort to change, do away with, avoid, or, alter our conscious challenges (experiences).

Example: If you go into work tomorrow and tell your boss to take the job and shove it, you have by your Freewill (conscious) created a challenge (experience) for your current life. Additionally, it is safe to say that you would never have done such a thing had you not allowed your emotions to escort the adjustment into your life.

EXPERIENCES WE MUST ENGAGE

However, some of the challenges (experiences) we encounter must be met void of our Freewill (conscious) effort to adjust or diminish them in any way. These are the challenges (experiences) from our Past Lives Records, determined during our Review Before Return Process. What we have sown, we shall reap!

The challenge (experience) may be physical, financial, or mental. It could be a relationship that goes awry, a job that we dislike, a difficult neighbor, the untimely death (or so we think consciously) of a love one, or any of the hundreds of difficult circumstances that may come into any of our lives.

Working as a professional psychic for thirty-plus years, I have come to understand that insight for Past Lives challenges (experiences) can be found in our current life expression. Help in understanding a particular challenge (experience) selected during our Review Before Return Process can be obtained through a "psychic reading," prayer and meditation, Past Life Regression, or in our dreams.

LEARNING TO LOOK FORWARD

Continually pondering the past is only a small part of the negative programming we learn which results in Twenty-twenty Blindsight as we go through life. We have all used the phrase "I realized" in our conversations.

Lately I have been substituting this phrase with "I admitted to myself." There is of course a reason that I have begun to incorporate this phrase into my conversations.

I believe from within my most Inner Being (Soul Mind)

that we came into this life with all of the answers contained within our Soul Minds. This wisdom includes those selections made during our Review Before Return Process. Clearly, we are here in this sojourn attempting to learn to blend the ego with the Spirit.

Every nuance of every individual must, at last, become blended with our Inner Spirit. Some beliefs that are being disseminated today favor the elimination of the ego altogether. This I disagree with vehemently. It is the blending of the ego and the Inner Spirit that is one of the primary requirements during our sojourn on the earth.

The subjugation of self (conscious) to their Inner Spirit must be relearned by many. Why would the ego exist though if it were intended that we do away with it? Who would sell, teach, train, be on radio, television or entertain us if the ego were suddenly discarded?

The many activities that we must become associated with while in physical (conscious) form, however, tend to shade over the Spiritual (Soul Mind) part of our lives if we are not ever mindful of our need for Spiritual balance.

PRAYER AND MEDITATION

The shading over of this balance can occur from our association with parents, organized dogma, friends, work environment, academia, etc. . . . It is therefore very important to remember to set aside a time for prayer and meditation each day. Prayer is talking to God, usually in an asking approach. Meditation is listening to God, connecting with our Soul Mind or Inner Spirit.

I often tell people to do nothing until they check with their Spirit (Soul Mind) first. The balance that is necessary in each and every one of our lives must be found through our own efforts to tap into that all-knowing energy that is often referred to as our Higher Minds, or Inner Spirit.

When we seek this balance, challenges (experiences) can be qualified, becoming growing experiences and we will at last comprehend that the balance is not external, but within.

MOVING BEYOND
OUR NEGATIVE PROGRAMMING

Additionally, it is extremely important that we realize that guilt, fear or control, whether self-imposed or inflicted on our lives by someone or something, is also exceedingly counter-productive. It is vital that we understand that the very point where we allow someone to change, by their input, the direction that we would take by our Freewill approach is the very place where our Spiritual Growth ceases to exist.

This type of input and response is also part of the negative programming I refer to as Twenty-twenty Blindsight. Spiritual Growth is an independent and individualized approach! Spirituality is therefore subjective, not objective.

In our effort to know God, we must continue to move forward into our future. Just imagine, if you will, attempting to travel down an unfamiliar road while constantly looking behind you. Of course the result would be disastrous. You see, life is really very much like traveling down an unfamiliar highway.

Before we set off for any given destination, we do not, as a common practice, recount all the unsavory driving experiences we have had to date. This would tend to cause great upset in our effort before we begin. So it is with our daily lives. We must look ahead and not behind, lest we run amok!

Do not for one moment think that I do not support learning from our past. However, there are many challenges (experiences) chosen in our Review Before Return Process, pertaining to our Soul Growth Issues, that we will not—cannot—consciously understand.

WHY GIVE THANKS FOR CHALLENGES

In faith we must be willing to give thanks for them. We must ask God to give us the wisdom to learn and grow from them. And we must leave the challenges where they belong, in the past! This will allow us to move into our future. Consciously over-analyzing the challenges (experiences) that are our Soul Growth Issues keeps us tethered to the past.

When we give thanks for a challenge (experience), past or present, we set a healing energy in motion that will accomplish three things for our Soul:

1. It will disallow the challenge (experience)
from controlling us emotionally.
2. It will disallow repetition of past challenges
(experiences) in our future.
3. It will connect our conscious thought to
our Soul Mind.

When we stumble and fall we should ask God to forgive us, ask others to forgive us if necessary and productive, forgive ourselves and begin again from where we are. If you have offended someone who you know will be hostile, present your petition to the universe, asking that anyone you have offended will forgive you.

Remember, Spirit communicates with Spirit. Even though you do not personally speak to the individual, the Universal Spirit of Love will take your message to that person in your stead.

Most of us have experienced a time when we have thought about someone for a few days, the phone rings, and there is the person we have been thinking about on the other end. Sometimes the person we have been thinking about shows up in our doorway.

Also, many times in our altered state of sleep we experience insight that pertains to someone we know who is alive, or perhaps in the Spirit realm. Such insights are excellent illustrations of Spirit communicating with Spirit.

Do not, day after day, no matter the circumstance, keep washing your face with the same dirty rag of the past. This would be most destructive to your future progress. Do not dwell on past mistakes when they cross your conscious mind.

MAKE THE FREEWILL CHOICE FOR POSITIVE THOUGHT

Remember, the human mind is inherently capable of having only one thought at any given moment. It is your responsibility to your Soul Development to keep your pathway (conscious mind) clear. If a negative thought crosses your path (conscious mind) do not dwell on it. You have a choice. You do not have to invite it in for tea or take it out to lunch. You have Freewill!

Repeat out loud, or to yourself if your prefer, a positive affirmation or a positive word with which to replace the negative thought (energy). In time, this will reprogram your conscious mind with an automatic positive thought process. The energy contained in this approach will begin to illuminate your pathway with a new understanding and bring to your life a *peace that passeth all understanding.*

Positive affirmations for prosperity, health, peace of mind, the healing of existing relationships, or for any healing you desire, should be repeated frequently in the initial phase of your efforts. This will prepare the foundation (thoughts, words and deeds) on which your future will rest.

It is your responsibility to consciously monitor these segments (thoughts, words and deeds) of your life each day. It is by your Freewill approach, making certain that your thoughts, words and deeds are positive, you will *co-create your future along with God each day.*

LIKE BEGETS LIKE

Understanding the concept of like begetting like is very important. This simply means that with your thoughts, with your words and with your deeds, you attract the future.

For example you may desire a healing for a particular relationship that seems to be difficult. If so, repeat just after waking, before rising in the morning and right before going to sleep at night the following: "God, it is my prayer that you will bring about a change between myself and (the person's name) for a more harmonious relationship."

Try it. You will, I am sure, be pleased with the results! Keep in mind that this is a very powerful prayer and tends to cut like a two edged sword.

Therefore, it is important that you realize before you say these words that the change can occur in you as well as the person that you designate in your prayer. Many a time, an individual has told me that after repeating this prayer twice a day for several weeks, they begin to see things in a much different light, *no longer controlled by Twenty-twenty Blindsight!*

3

CHOOSING THE DARK SIDE

I once told a former in-law that she was never happy unless she was miserable. Sound familiar? Why do some people seem to attract so much turmoil and suffering? An obvious response would be karma. Or perhaps you might think, "They are getting what they deserve."

A few years ago I overheard a friend tell her husband that he would never be happy. She further informed him she thought that misery seemed to run in his family. Patterns of grief, of one type or another, do seem to seek out certain families. The Kennedy and Clinton families come to mind.

Quite often, without our conscious awareness, Choosing The Dark Side has occurred layer upon layer, concept upon concept. As we make our way through life we begin to repeat what we have come to know and believe as truisms:

- Life is such a struggle.
- The good die young.
- They think they are better than we are.

- We are from the wrong side of the tracks.
- It's God's will.
- Suffering brings you closer to God.
- All great saints suffered tremendously.

The belief, still predominant today, that to suffer is to know God has been around for eons. Ultimately this thought process fosters the "need" for suffering. Unfortunately, suffering has been designated by many beliefs to indicate God's awareness of the person. When we subscribe to such a model of behavior, we begin to lay the foundation for Choosing The Dark Side of life.

It may be true that much of our grief in any life is karmic. Therefore, would it not follow that the grief we encounter in each life expression is deserved? Our Past Lives Record unquestionably is an etheric ledger that classifies our karma by "type of grief" that we must encounter in our present and subsequent lives.

How the Challenges in This Life Help Our Souls to Grow

However, it is my belief that this etheric ledger has a miscellaneous page that allows our Soul Mind to volunteer for a particular "type of grief" that majestically advances our Soul Growth. "Soul Grief Choices" are the Spiritual equivalent to writing a paper in college for extra credit. "Soul Grief Choices" are selected during the Review Before Return Process, exclusive of karma. Choices of this type "turbocharge" the advancement and elevation of our Soul Growth.

In other words, if during our previous lives we had Spiritually confronted and resolved all Past Lives Karma, reincarnation would not be required. Karma, in the idiom of this chapter, is debt repayment. A "Soul Grief Choice," like Soul Growth Issues, necessitates reincarnation. The latter is contained in our Past Lives Record, indicative of karma (debt repayment), while a "Soul Grief Choice" is not.

A few years ago, the mother of a seventeen-year-old daughter who had committed suicide came to see me. She also had two other children, a daughter who was sixteen and a son, fourteen.

The grief the woman was experiencing was consuming her entire life. She could not help but think that there must have been something she overlooked that could have helped her save her daughter's life. She kept questioning her fitness to be a good mother. She thought if she could not save her daughter who committed suicide, then she may not be able to protect her other two children

During our session I attempted to convey to the troubled mother a helpful way to consider challenges (experiences) that we encounter during our human sojourn. First we must determine what brought about the challenge (experience). Was there a conscious action on our part that brought the challenge (experience) into our lives? Or, as in her case, did the challenge (experience) manifest exclusive of conscious actions? I continued by explaining to her that these types of manifestations are Soul Growth Issues as well as "Soul Grief Choices." I also told her that Soul Growth Issues and "Soul Grief Choices" are easily identified.

They consist of any challenge (experience) that we did not choose consciously. Therefore, we cannot resolve them consciously. In other words, we do not have (consciously) the "for what reason knowledge" to deal with the challenge (experience) at hand. Consequently, these challenges (experiences) are a Soul Growth Issue or "Soul Grief Choice."

GIVING THANKS HEALS

These selections are made during The Review Before Return Process by our Soul Mind. Because they are chosen by our Spirit, we must heal them with our Spirit. In the human sojourn the mechanism by which this will be accomplished is a prayer of giving thanks.

I encouraged the grief-stricken woman to give thanks for this experience. She was very annoyed that I would suggest such a ludicrous response. I endeavored to explain the healing efficacy of giving thanks for challenges (experiences), but to no avail. After the session that day, my client reminded me as she left that giving thanks was not at all in the realm of possibilities for a mother who has lost her child.

Giving thanks for the challenge (experience) and asking for wisdom to learn and grow from it activates our Soul Mind and sets the Healing Energy in motion. This Healing Energy will accomplish three things pertaining to the current Soul Growth Issue or "Soul Grief Choice":

1) Giving thanks will disallow the challenge (experience) from controlling us emotionally (consciously).
2) Giving thanks will set aside repetition for future challenges (experiences). Similar (conscious) devastation cannot capture our lives in the present or subsequent sojourns.
3) Giving thanks will connect the conscious thought to the Spiritual Mind, time-releasing the purpose of the challenge (experience) as we are ready to "no longer see through the glass darkly."

Although I encouraged the grief-stricken mother as she left to please keep in touch, about six months passed before I heard from her. She called and said she was at her wit's end. She could not let go of the nagging thought that she should have been able to help somehow. As a result of this focus she had moved out of her home, leaving her other daughter, son and husband behind.

Through uncontrollable sobs she asked me to remind her of why I thought she needed to give thanks for this nightmare that had become her reality. I repeated what I had shared with her during her session. At the end of my explanation, she said, "I will give it a try. I have nothing else left, In fact, I have been so distraught that I have contemplated suicide myself." This was five years ago.

Today this same woman is a keynote speaker all over the country for parents whose children have taken their own lives. About three years after she began to counsel with other grief-stricken parents, she called to ask me if I thought God had taken her daughter so that she would do this work. I told her that I could not speak for God; however, I was certain that without this "Soul Grief Choice," she would not have very much to share on this topic.

I also told my client that it was my observation and interpretation of her vibration (energy field) that this was a "Soul Grief Choice," not a karmic incident. I felt an overwhelming awareness that her Soul Mind chose this experience, not for punishment or karma, but as an instrument of God's healing power.

Parents who must face the death of a child say it is the most painful experience known to humankind. It is thought (consciously) to be unnatural for the child to precede the parent in death.

THE LIMITLESS SOUL MIND

Nevertheless, we must remain attentive to the knowledge that the conscious mind is limited to what it has learned or been taught in any given life. The Soul Mind (Spirit Mind) is unlimited. The Soul Mind is a reservoir of information that pertains to our past, present and future. The Past Lives Record is only one facet of this information. The future information pertains to potentialities for the future. Limitless possibilities exist. Every thought possibility becomes a part of this record. Our conscious imagination (thought) is the energy (power) that adds to this record. Negative thoughts also become part of this record (reservoir). Our Freewill ignites the power of our thoughts, our words and our deeds. It is each person's individual responsibility to keep these areas of our human expression positive. In so doing, *we co-create our future along with God each day!*

WHY GIVING THANKS WORKS

Constant focus on the event that brings what we conceive (consciously) to be the negative challenge (experience) prohibits our Spiritual understanding and resolve. Moreover such focus prevents us from moving into our future.

Over the years I have observed that no matter the challenge (experience) the human psyche conditionally, for the most part, thinks the worst first. Whether it is the loss of a loved one, the loss of a job, a divorce, a health issue or any other unplanned challenge (experience) we seem to have a pervasive proclivity for fear-based (negative) thinking.

In all things, if we can just remember that like begets like, we can begin the process of healing.

So, when a challenge (experience) occurs that we (consciously) do not understand and we begin to whine, moan and groan about the circumstance, we add to the "perceived negativity" that already exists. Healing cannot occur from this approach.

By giving thanks we activate our Spiritual Mind (Soul Mind), allowing the healing to begin. Giving thanks will not suffice for the pain that a mother feels when a child dies. However, it will not allow the mother's focus on the loss to become more important than the future. Without knowing it, many people have allowed the pain of a personal loss (the value of that loss), whether a death, divorce, job, health, or other problem, to be exchanged for their limitless future.

Everyone will experience change. Spiritually it is destructive to not allow ourselves to think, speak and act beyond the point of a perceived loss. It is safe to say that most people, regardless of their religious background, believe the Soul lives on when we die. Only the body is set aside. With this perspective in mind, does it not stand to reason that the departed Soul is obstructed from further development in the Spirit realm by our extended or exaggerated grief?

GRIEVING POSITIVELY

After an acceptable grieving period has passed, each time we think of the departed loved one, we should call their name and tell them to "go toward the light." Otherwise our prolonged grief will keep the Soul of the departed loved one earthbound. This disallows the growth that is available and necessary in the Spirit Realm. Keeping the Soul earthbound denies the opportunity for reincarnation as well. Each Soul, after departing a human life, will be assisted by master teachers in the Spirit Realm.

Assessment of the most recent as well as previous lives prepares the Soul for further reincarnations if necessary. It is not unusual for Souls that are preparing for departure to be visited and greeted by previously deceased loved ones.

In each life expression our encounter with any Soul is diminutive in relationship to that Soul's Past Lives Record. Each of us is but a single element of the aggregate representation in the effort for that Soul to reconnect with God. Our prayers for the departed, calling them by name and telling them to "go toward the light," assist the departed Souls exceedingly with their Soul Growth Issues.

Be comforted in the knowledge that we tend to reincarnate in groups or waves of people with which we have previously been connected. The dynamics of our connection can vary from life expression to life expression. In other words, a daughter can become the mother in the subsequent life, or the best friend.

The current earth life challenge (experience) you have with neighbors, parents, children, co-workers, siblings, etc. is just one of the many potential encounters your Souls might have. The neighbor who irritates you with unreasonable demands is possibly the authority figure from a prior life whom you now can challenge. Anger, well placed, is not inappropriate to our Soul Growth. To live in anger day after day, of course, would be inappropriate. If we are to observe the Christ figure as an example to emulate, anger is acceptable. Did He not turn over the tables of the money changers in the temples?

FREEWILL CAN OVERCOME NEGATIVE THOUGHTS

Over the years, many clients have asked me if I thought this was their last life. I must admit that on more than one occasion I have found myself thinking, "I hope so, lest our paths cross again."

No matter how Spiritual we become, perfection of thought, word and deed can continue to elude us. Simply put, we must be human. At times the conscious mind will be continually deluged by unworthy thoughts. However, it is our Freewill responsibility to our Soul Growth not to allow the energy of these thoughts to be expressed. (The birds may fly over our heads, but we do not have to let them build a nest in our hair). In other words, we must replace this type of thought with one that is Spiritual.

Example: God, renew my Faith; help my unbelief. Refusal to entertain the energy of negative thoughts redefines the vibration around our lives and as such attracts the more favorable into our lives.

Thinking, speaking and acting negatively is one of the quickest ways to fracture our Spirits. So, why must we or why do we think the worst first when a challenge (experience) appears in our lives? We may say that it is conditioning. However, to recognize wrong simply means that it can no longer control or possess your life, UNLESS YOU ALLOW! Just the recognition of wrong means that we are on the way to becoming whole again. Our awareness is the ingredient with which to repair the fracture that fear-based thinking has produced in our Spirits.

Do not buy into the negative (fear-based thought) approach with each challenge (experience) that occurs in your life. The price you will pay is all too great! The Spiritual Energy (Vibration) around our lives can become so polluted with our negative thoughts, our negative words and our negative deeds that we cannot see the light of our future. When we reach this point in our lives, by thinking the worst first, we allow the negative energy to accumulate around us in such a manner that all we anticipate is more and more negativity. This type of approach culminates in Choosing The Dark Side.

4

TURNING
THE LITTLE CORNERS

From a conscious perspective, letting go of the past can be one of life's most complex and painful undertakings short of having a lobotomy or shock treatment. Unfortunately, many continue to hold on to the bitterness, hurt and confusion throughout their entire life. Over the years I have encountered many individuals who have had years of psychological therapy, grasping for self-identity. They were desperately hoping to find a way to cope with and ultimately alleviate the pain from their past.

Although many feel they have derived some tangible benefits from therapy, many also feel that the pain remains just beneath the surface. Remaining constantly on the alert, they are fearful that something someone might say, a smell, something they might see, will bring the pain of the past flooding back into their conscious minds, full force. This conscious (emotional) behavior pattern is, needless to say, absolutely fear-based.

However, various challenges (experiences) encountered in any given life have been chosen during the Review Before Return Process (by the Soul Mind), which implies a Soul Growth Issue or a Soul Grief Choice. For these, logic (conscious reflection) will not suffice. Other challenges (experiences) we encounter have manifested in the current life experience, entirely as an outgrowth of our thoughts, our words and our deeds!

From a Spiritual perspective, though, there is "hope to cope," as well as healing for the pain of the past! I will share more later in the chapter about the Spiritual approach.

However, let me first share a portion of my own life's journey. I share the following experience from my own personal life confident that it can inspire those who need to heal the past to begin from where they are.

The past was an area of my life with which I struggled for many years. Growing up in an abusive alcoholic environment had left scars of hatred and bitterness, which, for many years, tarnished the dynamics of interpersonal relationships in my own life.

Moreover, there was little in the way of what I call "show-ME's" or "go-by's" that I could use as a basis by which to prepare myself for the world as an adult. When I left home at seventeen, I would discover the world outside of my family environment was a total mystery to me.

Most people who grow up in a troublesome home environment are psychologically predisposed to develop a very defensive disposition early on in life. I, as well as my three siblings, lived a life that was torturous until we, each in our own way, left home. My mother, a very religious person, tried courageously to keep the family intact. Despite the seemingly insurmountable obstacles that tend to be the progeny of such a lifestyle, our family managed to portray a harmonious facade to family and friends.

A Haunting Past

My dad, an alcoholic, womanizing man, would disappear for weeks at a time. Frequently he would get into bar brawls, resulting in jail terms. It could take days for the legal authorities to notify my mother that she needed to come and get him out of jail. As a consequence of my dad's inability to read or write, we lived in various farm environments during my childhood.

Like many people tied to an agrarian lifestyle at that time, we were extremely poor. It would take a tremendous effort on our mother's part to scrape together enough money from relatives and friends to pay my dad's fines and get him out of jail.

During the time I lived at home, our family could not afford a phone. We lived in north Florida on a farm. My mother's relatives were scattered throughout southeast Georgia. During any given crisis mother would set out to bring some resolve to the circumstance. Her efforts could include but were not limited to writing letters to her family as well as asking the church we attended for assistance. This process could take quite a while—a week or more—to accomplish. We were so impoverished that on one occasion we could not find the three cents required to mail a letter.

Sometimes Dad would meet a woman in a bar, go off with her for a few days, and eventually find his way home. Each time he disappeared, we anticipated his return with great fear and trepidation. As soon as he was released from jail or kicked out by his woman of the evening, the drinking would resume.

At home he could be very violent, knocking all of us around, including our mother. He would beat us with his fist, a piece of wood, a hoe handle, his belt or anything he could get his hands on. When our mother tried to protect us from him, I can remember on several occasions he grabbed her by the throat or hair of the head and threw her across the room. He drank to such an extent that conscious recollection of these events was, as a rule, eradicated. If he had left one of us bruised and bleeding, the next day he would reluctantly ask what happened. Scenarios like this continued for years.

My mother, I believe, had a seventh-grade education. She was a very religious woman and would take us to church as much as she could. I think it would be fair to say that our mother was a religious extremist. Anyone who did not believe the way she did, right down to going to the same denomination of church, was doomed to hell. To save our souls, then, she endeavored to imbue her four children with this same doctrine!

Growing up, my siblings and I made an obligatory endeavor to appease our mother. "Sacrilegious," "agnostic," or "demonic in thinking" were but a few of the labels applied to children who dared to differentiate their thoughts from those of their parents when I was a boy.

In my adult life, however, by way of my Freewill, these prohibitive beliefs have faded into a welcome obscurity. In retrospect, I believe the focus my mother had on religion was literally "her salvation," considering the conditions in which we lived.

Mother did not learn to drive until after I did. I was around nine when, to my amazement, my dad taught me to drive a logging truck. The truck had nine forward gears and three reverse gears. Needless to say, my dad was not the most patient teacher. I would just sit in the truck for hours, practicing how to shift. Although my dad wanted to teach me, I did not want to do anything that would provoke his ire. My practicing paid off. My dad was amazed with my driving aptitude. I can recall only two other times that my dad said he was proud of me. Once was when the high school band in which I played won a state championship. I played a tenor saxophone. I was around fifteen or sixteen at the time. The other time happened when I won an art scholarship. Which, by the way, he would not let me accept. The scholarship issue came a few months before I left home.

Nevertheless, at the time I learned to drive my dad had no idea that I had spent hours practicing shifting the gears in the truck. I would wait until he had passed out, take the truck keys from his pocket, and go practice shifting the gears.

I did not start or drive the truck during these practice marathons. However, you had to have the key in the "on" position in order to shift the gears.

For several weeks I was excited that my dad wanted to teach me anything. Spending time with any of his four children was not customary for my dad. I later found out that his driver's license had been suspended because of his many drunk driving episodes. The judge had told him if he was caught driving for a period of six months, he would serve time behind bars.

In the early '50s, Dad purchased a Chevrolet sedan that was to be our family car, or so he said at the time. For most of my growing-up years we had pick-ups, logging or dump trucks. And, as it turned out, we did not keep the car very long. A few months later, he traded that car in for one that had an automatic transmission.

About the time Dad bought the car with the floor shift, Mother decided she was tired of being stranded at home and totally dependent on our dad. She wanted to learn to drive. Shortly after he had brought the car home, he disappeared again. That did it. Mother decided she must to learn to drive. After all, we lived several miles out in the country. And here she was, stranded, with four small children, all of them under the age of twelve.

So, the process of learning to drive began for my mother.

I was the only one of the four children who would ride with her. My sister and two brothers were extremely apprehensive. Hence, Mother and I left them at home and set off down the dirt road in front of our house in the old sedan.

Mother was having a terrible time with the floor shift. I don't believe that she ever got the car out of first gear, though she tried valiantly to do so. In fact, she was so busy trying to figure out how to shift that she failed to notice that we were headed right for the ditch. It had rained the day before and the sides of the ditch were very slick. In the area where we lived there was a lot of red clay. When clay gets wet it can be difficult for a seasoned driver to control a vehicle, much less a beginner. Needless to say, by the time Mother realized we were headed for the ditch, it was too late. We wound up with the front end of the car down in the ditch and the rear end sticking up close to the graded road.

My mother was not about to be undone. She was accustomed to dealing with unfavorable circumstances. She told me to run back to the house and get the logging truck. We would use that to pull the car out of the ditch. Excited, I ran the mile or so to the house and drove the logging truck back.

Well, wouldn't you know it—we got that stuck, too. We never stopped to think about our inexperience in driving a vehicle, much less our lack of knowledge or experience in pulling one vehicle out of a ditch with another vehicle. When I was growing up we were in the habit of just doing, until something did not work. Preplanning for adversities was not in our way of thinking. It was a struggle each day just to live, much less to plan! Day in and day out, the work of surviving left little time for anticipating problems that might or might not occur.

Exasperated, my mother now decided I should go and get the tractor. Never doubting my mother's plan, I ran off in the direction of our house to get the tractor. Just about the time

I was running up to the barn to get the tractor, my dad came home.

We were all terrified that he would fly off the handle and beat the hell out of everyone.

That would have been the typical reaction for him. However, for some reason that no one understands to this day, he saw the humor in the whole fiasco. Before long, he set about getting the truck and car out of the ditch.

At any rate, after this incident, my mother was convinced she had learned to drive. Never mind that she could not shift the gears. Never mind that she wound up in the ditch during her one and only attempt at driving. She had learned to drive! From that day forward when my dad would leave, she would pile us all in the car and head off to town or church, depending on the day of the week. For the longest time we drove to and from town, about fourteen miles, in one gear.

Mother could not parallel park, even when the car had a reverse gear. Dad had stripped out the reverse gear in the car while trying to pull a truck out of a ditch during one of his drunken episodes. She was not great at stopping either.

After the towing episode, we had to park head-on, at a slight angle, as most parking was in those days in small rural towns. When we were ready to leave, we four kids would have to push the car backwards out of the parking space. Parking spaces in those days were designed to have a downward slope, toward the sidewalk. I have often reflected on the degree of incline of that slope.

At the time it felt like we were trying to push the car backwards up Mount Rushmore! Mother would get in the car and steer while we four kids would push until we cleared the vehicles on both sides. Then we would quickly get in, praying fervently that none of our school friends had seen us.

The parking issue coupled with the extreme rocking and jerking back and forth while mother tried to shift gears embarrassed my sister immensely. She used to tell our mother that it was a full time job just keeping herself upright. Should she see anyone she knew, my sister would make a futile attempt to hide.

The church we attended at the time had a huge oak tree out near the parking area. I can remember on several occasions that mother would head straight for that tree while she was trying to figure out how to stop the car. She had a difficult time trying to coordinate the clutch, the floor shift and the brakes. On more than one occasion she allowed the car to roll into the tree to bring us to a stop.

Often we could not go anywhere, though. During my dad's frequent bouts of drunkenness he would usually take the distributor cap or a few of the spark plugs out of the car to keep us from going anywhere. When he did this, we were stranded for days at a time.

My dad was continually on the look-out for some type of "get-rich-quick scheme." One of the many wild schemes that my dad involved our family in was okra. Yep, after conferring with all of his drinking cohorts as well as his girlfriend at the local farmers' market, he got it in his head that okra was the money crop that year. Consequently he planted several acres.

Keep in mind, now, that my dad did not intend to pick the okra. His idea was that my mother, my sister, and I would do that. We did. Mother would put a blanket under a tree at the end of the rows on which my two younger brothers were to sit and play. My mother, my sister, and I picked okra until our hands bled.

Okra is covered with fine fuzz. Extended exposure to this fuzz with bare hands will cause bleeding. We pleaded with him to buy us some gloves. Repeatedly he said no. After watching our hands bleed for several days, he acquiesced and came back from town one day with rubber gloves.

We were elated. Alas, though, our excitement was short-lived. If only he had bought good ones. Instead he bought the cheapest kind he could find. It took only two days for the flimsy gloves to tear and begin to fall apart. We picked okra from sun-up to sun-down. The gloves he bought were for doing dishes or some other light household chore.

Rubber dishwashing gloves are not made for working hour after hour in the fields. Nevertheless he refused to buy us any other kind. He thought they were too expensive. Keep in mind, he was spending all day in the bar drinking or with his girlfriend at the farmer's market, while my mother, my sister, and I spent all day in the fields.

On several occasions while we were growing up, my dad, in his drunken stupor, would try to molest my sister. With one exception, we hid this from our mother all of her life. One time, though, I ran several miles to the restaurant where my mother worked to tell her. Mother started to work as a cook in a restaurant when my sister and I were around twelve and thirteen. When we got back, my dad beat all of us, including my mom when she demanded to know what was going on. He choked me until I said I had made it up. I never told again.

My sister is two days shy of a year older than me. She was born May 19, in 1943. I was born May 17, 1944. We have a brother three years younger than me and another six years younger than me.

As the oldest child, my sister at a very early age was made to feel she was responsible for us three boys. I have always said my sister was born old. She has always seemed so "strong." She has told me in later years that she was not so strong at all. She was just scared. She was afraid not to act unfeeling!

I, on the other hand seemed to be more happy-go-lucky and outgoing. I had an Inner Peace that I was protected. Even as a small child, I would tell my mother that three angels were protecting me. I have always been aware of a bright light of protection undulating around me, even in early childhood.

For the most part, my life remained an unrelenting series of similar episodes. I am sharing just a few, though, enough for you to understand my journey.

My sister and I were in our mid-teens when we began to fight back. I think it all began when our mother tried to commit suicide.

One night we became aware that our mother was not in the house. As my sister ran out the front door, she yelled that mother had made a statement earlier that evening that she was "just going to just step out in front of the next big truck that came down the road and end it all." I ran down the lane after my sister. Mother was standing by the road, just staring out into space. My sister talked to her, but she was not responding.

She appeared to be in a trance-like state. I saw my mother in this dazed state one other time in my life. I was in my late twenties when I got a call from my sister one day that Mother had run Dad out of the house with a butcher knife. She had caught him staring flirtatiously and chatting passionately with our neighbor. The neighbor lady was in the habit of wearing short shorts while she did yard work. When I got there, mother was sitting at the table in the kitchen with that same dazed look in her eyes.

The night that mother was going to commit suicide, my sister and I took her by the arms and led her back in the house. From that point forward my sister and I started to fight back. Initially, we tried to reason (argue) with our dad, while projecting a brave front. Within a couple of years we became so bold that we would actually try to grab him and hold on when he would start to become violent. He was usually so drunk when we did this that it was not difficult to restrain him. His equilibrium was usually nil.

Over the years my sister and I repeatedly encouraged our mother to leave our dad. She always believed that he would change. Her religious belief taught that marriage vows were forever. Later in life, she said she was terrified at the thought of leaving him while we were young.

She was afraid she could not raise four kids by herself. All she knew how to do to earn money was to be a cook. She did not feel she had enough education to support a family of five.

When my mother died, her oldest sister told me that their daddy was just like mine. A lot of the puzzle suddenly made sense. Like begets like!

As my dad got older, he quit drinking and carousing. Fearful of death, he "joined the church." When he died February 29, 2000, he still had no close relationship with his four children, his grandchildren or great-grandchild. I believe he may have seen his great-grand-child once before his death.

In July of 1999, I told my sister, one brother, and an aunt that I felt Dad would die in February or March of 2000.

In telling them, I had hoped to provide the impetus to help heal the past. My siblings and I had tried on many occasions prior to my warning of his death to redefine the relationship with our dad. But he was never willing to talk about the past. If it was mentioned, he denied doing anything wrong.

The denial of past actions serves to impede any attempt to heal. As long as responsibility is denied, there is no basis for a healing to begin. Once responsibility is accepted, a plan of change must follow. My dad refused to accept responsibility his entire life.

In December of 1993, I told my sister, my two brothers, and one of my mother's sisters who lived in the same town that Mother was going to die in July or August of 1994. She died August 16, 1994.

I attended my mother's funeral. I did not attend my dad's. Some people who read this book will think I should have gone to my dads' funeral no matter what. Other people will think that if he was the way I have portrayed him, then they don't blame me for not going.

UNDERSTANDING GOD'S LOVE
BRINGS FREEDOM FROM THE PAST

Allow me to share with you what some of my thoughts have been and what some of my thinking is today. I will start with saying that I when I left home at seventeen, I thought I had figured out five different ways to kill my dad and not get caught. Or, so I thought. Enumerating them now would be pointless.

The reason I left home at seventeen? There are many. I have shared only a few. However, the day I left home, I had shoved my dad off the front porch. I had done this to keep him from hitting my brother, who is three years younger than me, with a thick leather strap again. He had knocked my brother down, put his foot on his neck and was violently beating him with a heavy leather strap. When I pushed him off the front porch, he ran to a tool room at one end of the porch and grabbed a crowbar. He lunged at me, yelling that he was going to bust my brains out. I jumped off the porch, out into the yard and ran down the lane in front of the house.

I had run about a quarter of a mile when I heard my dad yell that he was going to kill me. And then I heard this loud ka-boom! He had fired both barrels of a double-barreled shot gun. A neighbor who lived about three miles up the road from us told me this a few weeks later when our paths crossed in town.

To this day I do not know whether my dad shot at me or shot into the air. Either is possible, I suppose. However, I do know that such memories can decay inside of you in a way that the byproduct produced by this decay will become a toxin to your very Soul.

I lived with this decay until my early forties. Not until then did I realize that the relationship I had with my dad was one of my Soul Growth Issues. As such, I did not know that embracing the pain, giving thanks for it, and asking for wisdom to learn and grow from it would elevate my Soul.

I grew up in the South. I saw people who called themselves Christians and "religious" treat African-Americans, Jews or any other person "different" from them with hatred and duplicity. I had a relative who was a high-ranking official in the town where he lived, and who also owned and operated moonshine stills. I had a relative who professed to be in the poorhouse all the many years that he was a preacher. When he died his widow and children "discovered" certificates of deposit worth hundreds of thousands of dollars in the bank.

Several of my relatives have had illegitimate children. More than one professed preacher in my family has run off with a younger woman or man. Men as well as women could be preachers in the church my mother attended. When a preacher ran off with someone, this would tend to really heat up things! Any such event fueled gossip for many months. Other relatives have divorced their spouses for someone else.

I would look on in disbelief as people who called themselves "religious" or "Christians" would turn their backs on these relatives. My dad, mother and two brothers disowned my sister when she left her first husband. They refused to have anything to do with her for more than two years.

I was always puzzled that one could be "judged so harshly for their sins." They would be disowned! Interestingly, there is no record of Jesus, Mohammed, Buddha or any other great prophet judging or condemning anyone.

When I was around sixteen, a friend and I were called before the church council for going to the prom. Dancing wasn't allowed! Neither was coloring your hair. So, when my friend and I appeared before the "Council" and were told that we had to stand up in the next service and apologize to the church, my friend's response surprised me.

She said, "Fine, we will do this as long as the preacher's wife apologizes to the church for dying her hair blue." Needless to say, we were dismissed posthaste. We were informed on our way out that "God would not be pleased if we spoke of what had transpired in our meeting outside of those walls."

These are but a few of the influences I had been exposed to when I left home at seventeen. I had always understood from deep within my Inner Being that Spirituality is how we treat one another. All else is theory. I believed that regardless of color, ethnicity or religious belief, we were all the same Spiritually. Growing up in the south I was exposed to many prejudices. I was never comfortable with prejudice. I was very aware of it, but tried to ignore it. Living in a predominately white Anglo-Saxon part of the country, with a dose of redneck thrown in at the time, it wasn't healthy to be free-thinking.

People who stepped out of line were often found beat up real bad or dead. Fortunately since my childhood, there has been something of an awakening in the world. I continue to pray for the day, when all hatred and prejudice will be abolished.

Gender, race, and religious belief can not be individualized in the Spirit Realm. There is only LOVE! Visitations from departed loved ones while we are still in human form can only be experienced using an anthropological identity form. Once the soul has made the transition from the physical to the Spiritual Realm, anthropological identity does not exist. As an example, if a mother and child expired simultaneously, recognition in the Spirit Realm would be through familiarity of Spirit only; not as mother and child.

Spirit identifies with Spirit. The Soul of the child would not be known as the son, or daughter. When a person expires, anthropological identity is assigned to the Past Lives Record, not the eon-to-eon experience and identification of the Soul in the Spirit Realm.

Beliefs are germane to the human expression. As we pass through the door from our physical life to our Spiritual Life, the belief systems pertinent to the human life expression are set aside. There is only LOVE! Truth is germane to the Spirit!

A misnomer often occurs in the human form when individualized beliefs are called "the" truth! Truth is subjective. Freewill is the spark that fosters Soul Growth. In each human life expression, the thoughts, the words and the deeds are the foundation on which the future sits. It is each person's Freewill responsibility to monitor his or her thoughts, words and deeds.

5

FREEDOM FROM THE PAST

Fast-forward to my early forties and the summer of 1991. Freedom from my past began one day when I was on my way home after going to visit my dad's half-brother. We had never been allowed to know him while we were growing up. He was illegitimate. Can you imagine the struggle of seeing the wrong of illegitimacy when held up against the backdrop of my life? I could have done illegitimacy with both hands tied!

Over the years, I have seen many people ostracized for the so-called wrongs that they have committed. Personally, I have never been able to turn my back on or disown anyone for any real or imagined indiscretion. I used to think that being crippled, blind, or deaf would have been better than what I had endured in my early years.

The conscious mind in human form is limited. Wisdom *from a conscious perspective* is only that which we have learned or have been taught in any given life. Wisdom *from a*

Spiritual perspective is a cumulative (life after life) harmonizing energy, culminating in pure love.

Back to the visit with my illegitimate uncle. When I pulled up in his driveway, my uncle came out to greet me. I could not believe my eyes. He looked just like my grandfather who had passed away a few years previously. There was no denying this relative.

I must say I enjoyed our visit tremendously. I met first cousins who I did not know existed. Some were Hispanic and half Anglo. As an aside, I also have relatives who are half African American and half Anglo in another branch of the family. We have Irish, Cherokee Indian and German blood, too, in the family soup. And who knows what else?

While my uncle and I visited, he mentioned that he and my dad had talked about a year before. My dad told him that I was living in Phoenix, Arizona, and doing the devil's work. My uncle went on to tell me that my dad felt that working as a psychic in the media, working with the legal authorities around the country, and seeing clients privately was an unacceptable way for me to earn a living. I should go back into accounting. My dad felt I was throwing away my college education as well as twenty-five years of respectable experience.

During my dad's entire life, he was unaware that I had been doing psychic work since I was nineteen. Beginning in the late '60s, I had been working with legal authorities on missing person and homicide cases. As a young man, I figured what he didn't know wouldn't hurt me.

He certainly did know, however, that around the age of eight I began to tell my parents things that I would "see." After several of the incidents came to pass, my parents became anxious and uncomfortable when I would begin to share an insight about the future. One night when I was around sixteen, I awoke with a vision of my mother's oldest brother. He was very sick. In the vision I saw him bleeding from his mouth as well as his rectum.

I was so shaken by what I saw that I awakened my mother around midnight to tell her of the vision. It was many years later when my uncle died. However, what I had seen in my vision came to pass.

On another occasion, my dad was going to talk to a man about a job. My mother and I were going with him. I was sitting in the back seat. As my dad started to get out of the car, I blurted out, "There is no need for you to go inside; you won't get the job." This infuriated my dad. He turned around and backhanded me so hard that the impact of his slap cut my lip.

He went inside to inquire about the job. It was only two or three minutes before he returned, frantically blaming me for the outcome. He said he felt like beating me until I could not speak.

So, although my father may not have known how long I had been working as a psychic professional, both parents had known of my psychic abilities since I was a child. Too often, they had reacted to my glimpses of the future with fear and anger.

While driving back to Phoenix after the visit with my new-found uncle, I was really struggling with feelings of hate and anger for my dad. I stopped at a rest stop along the way to use the facilities. When I got back in my car I sat with my head resting on my arms, which I had folded over the steering wheel.

I sat there for a few minutes and silently prayed, asking God to please help me release all the bitterness and hatred I felt for my dad. All of a sudden I felt the most incredible energy of love. I became aware of a presence that begins to convey thought-energy to me.

It was conveyed to me that unless I embraced my past, gave thanks for the experience, and asked for wisdom to learn and grow from that experience, I would repeat it again in a subsequent life. It was also conveyed that I would encounter the same people in the subsequent life experience that I had encountered in this life.

Through this conveyance, I was impressed with an understanding that when we give thanks for our adversities, we set a healing energy in motion that will accomplish three things which will explicitly benefit and enhance our Soul Growth:

1. Giving thanks will disallow the experience from controlling us emotionally.
2. Giving thanks will prevent repetition of the same experience in subsequent lives.
3. Giving thanks connects the conscious mind to the Spiritual Mind.

It was also conveyed by thought-energy that *like* is a conscious expression. Love is a Spiritual expression. Consciously I did not have to "like" my father. Therefore, I did not have to be around him, consciously. Spiritually, I had to pray for him. Prayer is Spirit Love.

Suddenly it became crystal-clear to me that I could heal the past with love. It didn't matter at that moment that I did not have the know-how to place love against the past on my own. I knew that in human form (consciously) I was incapable of accomplishing this.

Yet, how was I to be free from my past as long as I was incensed by its very memory? Silently, I asked God to remove all the bitterness, the hurt and the pain of my past from my current life. Suddenly, I no longer saw "through the glass darkly." I knew from deep within my Inner Being that my past, including the experience with my dad, was indeed one of my "Soul Growth Issues" in this life. For this I gave thanks.

I also asked God to surround my dad with light and love,

and give him wisdom of thought and choice each day. That day, I was able to forgive my dad!

Sitting there, I did not see a bright light. There was no loud noise. No chariot or host of angels materialized, either. There was, however, an emerging peace in my Inner Spirit as well as my conscious mind that began to manifest from this newly conveyed knowledge.

From that day to this if I reflect on the past, if I refer to the past in conversations or if I write about it, I remember that now I KNOW that IT CANNOT

1. Control me emotionally
   IT WILL NOT
2. Be repetitive in my subsequent lives.
   AND
3. My conscious thought will be made wise through by my Spiritual Mind.
   For I HAVE given thanks... That is
   ALL that I am required to do!
   Love heals. God is Love.

In March of 2000, I went to Florida for a meeting with my siblings. It had been almost six years since I attended my mother's funeral. With the death of our dad, it was time to talk about our parents' estate. That was the last time my siblings and I were together. For the most part we have always been cordial to one another over the years. My three siblings all live in a small town in northern Florida. Like most families living close together, disagreement among the three has been known to occur. Very little disharmony has occurred between me and my siblings over the years.

Perhaps due to geographical proximity. Perhaps. However, since I was the executor of the estate, I said a prayer on the plane trip over to Florida that God would bring about harmony for everyone concerned.

In my opening statement during our family meeting, I did say that I did not like my dad and that I did not love him as a father, but I loved him because he was my father. I was thankful that I was able to heal the past on the trip back to Phoenix from the visit with my uncle, many years earlier.

HOW GIVING THANKS
FREES US FROM THE PAST

Realizing that other people's judgment did not have to be my compass in life was extraordinary! Finally, I had come to a place in my existence where the peace I felt within my Inner Spirit, (Higher Self, Spirit Mind, and Soul Mind) reflected the Spiritual lesson that I alone was to know from my experience with the past. *It is true for everyone. Your truth is Spiritually subjective.*

Matters not what we have experienced in our past, giving thanks will heal it. Consciously we can spend endless hours, weeks, months or even years regarding the wrongs that we felt were visited upon our life. This will keep the past alive, assisting in the deterioration of our Spiritual balance and the holding back of our positive future. Like begets like. *Contemplatively focusing on the past transposes (repeats) that energy into our future.*

Stop and consider. You cannot change the past. It was an experience, NOT a way of life. Only YOU make it so, by reflecting on it over and over again. *To decry our past or present challenges (experiences) only adds to the pain that we have already endured, exaggerating the "time-spent" requirement for that specific Soul Growth Issue.*

The wisdom of this began to influence my conscious awareness in my early forties. This wisdom has only been enhanced by my efforts of prayer and meditation. Remember, the Spirit Mind is All-Knowing. The Conscious Mind is limited to what it has learned or been taught in any given life!

If I can give thanks for my past and gain Spiritual Insight from the experience, I know you can as well. Try it. It works! It is important to put things in perspective. For instance, I know that my future is unlimited. *The only thing between me and my future is an attitude.* If I change my attitude I will change my future. Our life will chase after our thoughts. Our thoughts will not chase us down the street!

Second, we must stop and evaluate each circumstance that we consider a stumbling block in our path. Assess its "value." Does it have a mental value, an emotional value, or can we measure it with the dollar sign? Once we have made the assessment, we must then look upon the "value" and ask ourselves: Are we willing to trade our unlimited future for such a paltry (known) sum?

Why linger around the past? It is an energy that has already been emotionally spent. Simply giving thanks for the past and realizing that your entire life expression is all about growth, not about blame, will result in Soul Development. Our past consists of lessons in which we reacted emotionally rather than Spiritually.

TURNING THE CORNERS

So, wouldn't you agree that having already been there, done that, these are indeed the little corners? These are the consciously familiar corners that we must Spiritually turn.

Conscious familiarity (repetitive experience) will bring Spiritual growth only when we learn to give thanks and ask for the wisdom to learn and grow from all circumstances of our lives, past or present.

Today you can make a decision. How much of yourself are you willing to leave behind? If you continue to focus on the past, you are not moving into your future. You are in essence leaving the greater part of yourself in the past! The past was an experience, not a way of life. Not unless YOU make it so!

Consider the following model for "Compartmentalizing Your Energy" as a starting point in apportioning your conscious energy each day.

COMPARTMENTALIZING YOUR ENERGY:

- You MUST devote a minimum of 51 percent of your conscious energy to the future. This includes your Spiritual Focus, Meditation, Creative Endeavors and Personal Renewal Time (vacations). This is FIXED energy.
- Twenty percent of your conscious energy should be allocated to your relationships.
- Fifteen percent of your conscious energy should be allocated to your employment.
- Ten percent of your conscious energy should be allocated for unexpected events.
- Four percent of your conscious energy should be allocated as Flexible.

Not too long ago, I was telling a client that he must give thanks for the abuse that he had suffered at the hand of his father during his childhood. His reply was that he could not, because to him this would imply that it was all right, what his dad had done to him.

I assured him this was not the case. In fact, I reminded him that what his dad had done was not about blame; it was about growth! His, my client's growth! I reminded him that he (his Soul Mind) had chosen his father, and he had chosen his gender and his race. This was achieved during the Review Before Return Process.

He had also chosen the experience of discord in the family setting. His choice was, in fact, self meeting self. Or, you might say, debt repayment from a previous incarnation. Therefore his choice was in keeping with his Soul Growth

Issues.

As I have explained in a previous chapter, I believe that we choose the environments we come through for a purpose that is not always linked to karma. These choices are Soul Grief Choices. From a personal perspective, I know that I have helped many release the pain of past family issues by drawing on my own personal experience.

We can textbook an issue to death. We can look on as someone we know goes through a trying time and conjecture as to what actions we would take. However, we should all take care not to judge. Until we have walked in their shoes, our knowledge remains conscious, NOT Spiritual.

6

LESSONS THAT ARE BLESSINGS

EARLY CHALLENGES CAN STAY WITH US

M any times the indoctrination we endure in the formative years leaves an acrimonious imprint in our vibrations, a bitter taste. It can take many years for individuals to express their own lives, using their Freewill as the means by which to accomplish this. *Consequently, patterns of energy on which an individual imprinted during the formative years can harass the adult life, until the effort is made to redefine the vibration.*

We do not have to be miserable. However, at times it seems awfully convenient and easy. Quite often, during a particularly stressful period, we will mimic the behavior patterns that we imprinted on during our formative years.

In a knee-jerk response, we will exhibit energy patterns just like those expressed by our parents. These patterns of energy may have been extremely disturbing for us in our formative years. Still, here they are spilling out of our lives, into the lives of others. How could this be? How could we?

The answer to this situation is simpler than you might think. Consider. *If our parents were prone to making us feel guilty in our childhood, it was an experience our Soul chose during The Review Before Return Process.*

How to Grow
beyond Negative Thoughts

True, we may say we hated being treated that way, and vow to never act accordingly to our loved ones. But hate is a negative force. *Hate is presented in as well as through our belief systems.* Since like begets like (brings forth the same), we have cultivated a negative force, which we will harvest and give out by way of our emotions.

When emotions and stress collide in our lives, flashbacks of behavior patterns can come spilling out of our energy, causing a repetitive Soul Growth Issue or Soul Grief Choice experience.

By harboring hate for anything or anyone, we make provisions for a negative response. Suppressing imprints of behavior patterns from our formative years, will deny healing and advancement in our Soul Growth Issues and Soul Grief Choices. It is not about blame; it is about growth. *We must embrace and give thanks for all of the misery we have known if we are to have healing IN our Souls.*

The astrological influences that were in place at the time of our birth, the families, the race, the gender and the ideology imparted during our formative years, ALL–each and every facet of our being–were chosen by our Soul, during The Review Before Return Process.

These things define our Soul Growth Issues and Soul Grief Choices. *When we whine, moan or groan about our earth-life experiences, we are keeping alive the very energy patterns that we denounce.*

These suppressed imprints will attach to our lives, repetitious in their influence. *The expression of these patterns can only be silenced and healed by our embrace and the giving of thanks.*

COMPLAINING REINFORCES SUFFERING

Soul Growth Issues as well as Soul Grief Choices are not always monumental in their scope. They can be as simple as something that is annoying. So, put down the martyr and victim's hammer and chisel. For an explanation, let's talk briefly about the guilt issue as it pertains to a possible Soul Growth Issue or Soul Grief Choice.

You may say that it annoyed you when your mother or father tried to make you feel guilty during your formative years. But just the act of dwelling on the annoyance aggravates it. Your thought energy of whining, moaning and groaning will rehabilitate, *restoring to its former state,* the annoyance in your vibration.

As it pertains to our Soul Growth Issues or Soul Grief Choices, the annoyance is not important. It is our response to the annoyance that will determine if we have grown Spiritually. *Hence, imprints of emotional patterns of energy must be redefined.*

THINK TWICE
BEFORE "RESCUING" OTHERS

Often we are so conditioned by the indoctrination during our formative years that our responses are often expressed without much thought. Most everyone has been taught that compassion is a good thing. Following this type of thinking one would assume that if compassion prompted them to assist someone in need that had to be a good thing. Right?

Perhaps not. *For you as an observer, consciously assessing the plight of someone in need does not reveal to you the individual's Soul Growth Issues or Soul Grief Choices.* Getting involved in someone's challenge may interfere with an issue they chose during their Review Before Return Process for the current life, which had the potential to enhance their Spiritual Development.

Prayer and Meditation will assist in whether and how much you should become involved. *Before eagerly rushing in to give advice or money, ask in a Prayerful Meditative state if is it appropriate for you to intervene.*

What a blessing when we learn to listen to that inner voice. In the human experience, it may take several attempts to learn the value of such guidance. *It usually takes the human psyche crashing impetuously into a few trials and tribulations before the effort of listening is accomplished.*

Rushing in to apply compassion to another person's life without a Prayerful Meditative Approach is like playing Russian Roulette with both Souls. Interference with an issue chosen during The Review Before Return Process will cause our efforts to fall on fallow ground. *Codependency in its purest form is established between the two individuals. Our efforts are transformed from a gift out of our hand, to a debt for our Soul.*

It would be wonderful to learn to go within, listening to that inner guidance, at an early age. However, it usually takes most of us until we are in our forties to develop a sense of inner connection. Until that time most of us will be prone to echo what we have been indoctrinated to believe is true.

On one hand, Freewill seems to demand several years of experience in order to be utilized with confidence. On the other hand, it is important to understand that most of our Soul Growth Issues as well as Soul Grief Choices will be recognized and experienced during the formative years.

What accounts for the gap between our formative years and our early forties? *Ego! This is the byproduct of the beliefs that we chose to experience during our Review Before Return Process.* The egocentric belief that until we prove things logically and scientifically as it applies to our lives, we are without help or hope.

Amazing! The conscious Mind is limited to what it has learned or been taught. The Soul Mind is unlimited! Our Help AND Hope are Within! *You make the choice!*

7

SOUL-TO-SOUL
RESUSCITATION

R esuscitate: To revive, bring back to life, cure, heal, reanimate, bring around or revivify.

In each life expression (reincarnation), we are involved in a continual process of re-balancing our Souls. Individuals with whom our Spirit (Soul Mind) chose to reincarnate play a vital role in this re-balancing. For the most part, challenges that our Spirit (Soul Mind) has chosen to encounter during any given life are nothing less than a spotlight on a Soul Imbalance that needs to be addressed.

These choices are made by our Soul Mind during the Review Before Return Process. However, as mentioned in an earlier chapter, these choices may consist of Soul Growth Issues (implying karma) or Soul Grief Choices. The latter choice does not involve the Past Lives Records; therefore, karma is not implied.

A Soul Grief Choice provides the mechanism by which

God's Love will be demonstrated in an earthly environment. Further, Soul Grief Choices are invariably characteristic of the societal need(s) into which the Soul reincarnates.

CHALLENGES (EXPERIENCES) AND RESPONSIBILITIES

Soul Growth Issues and Soul Grief Choices are the sum and substance of our Soul Growth and Soul Advancement, respectively. It is fundamental for our Soul Development that we understand our challenges (experiences) are not about blame, but rather are about Soul Growth and Soul Advancement!

"Soul-Self Responsibility" is primary to our Soul Development endeavors. Complex challenges (experiences) during the human sojourn do not depict the judgments of a vengeful God being ruthlessly dispensed against an unloved Soul!

Likewise, the accountability for the people who are encountered during any life expression is from "Soul-Self Responsibility."

"Soul-Self Responsibility" is perpetually linked to the Past Lives Record of each Soul. "Soul-Self Responsibility" is debt repayment. Correspondingly, "Soul-Self Responsibility" is karma.

As long as we seek to make others culpable for our Spirit (Soul Mind) choices, we cannot accomplish Soul Growth or Soul Advancement. If we whine, moan and groan about the challenge (experience), whether it is a person, place or condition, we heal nothing. We add to the perceived negativity that already exists.

DEALING WITH STUMBLING BLOCKS

To be sure, we will encounter that which we define as oppositions, aggravations and stumbling blocks. So it is when our Spirit (Soul) occupies an anthropological form. In the human form we are Body, Mind AND Spirit.

Yet until we learn to give the Spirit attendance in our daily lives, the (conscious) human (Body and Mind) will tend to focus more on the oppositions, aggravations and stumbling blocks. Primarily this results from the connection between the conscious mind and the emotions, while we are in the human form.

Additionally, various methods by which our human psyche has been conditioned promote the illusion that the more emotional something is, the more believable it is.

We absolutely must understand that it is not the opposition, the aggravation, or the stumbling block that provides any measure of Soul Development for our lives. It is our *attitude in response* to these "experiences" that will provide the Soul Development that we need, and, by evidence of our existence in human form, for which we have contracted.

It is not wrong to analyze an "experience" encountered in a life expression. It is however, counterproductive in our pursuit of Soul Development to allow ourselves to worry or become fearful. Faith and fear cannot abide side by side. "Experiences" that we encounter—people or events, good or bad—provide the very basis of our Soul Development.

WHAT ARE SOUL GROWTH ISSUES AND SOUL GRIEF CHOICES?

It is quite easy to identify a Soul Growth Issue or a Soul Grief Choice. Simply put, it is anything, person or event, for which a conscious resolution cannot be found.

Example: Your relationship with your significant other suddenly comes to an abrupt end when the announcement is made that he or she has found someone else.

In this situation, it would not be unusual to agonize day and night over why and how this could have happened to you. After all, have we not been conditioned for eons to try to "figure things out?"

There must be a reason, or so we have been told! Alas,

before we forget the basic tenets of Soul Development, let us stop and lay hold of a few simple facts. Analyze, yes. Worry or fear, no! All relationships, no matter how difficult, are about Soul Development, not about blame.

FACILITATING SOUL DEVELOPMENT

We must remember that the ending of a relationship will not provide Soul Development. Soul Development is determined by *the way* any relationship, family, friend, work environment, or living environment is brought to that place of change. The following approach can be very useful when in the future you face a challenge (experience) for which you do not have the answer.

Step One: Analyze the "experience." If you find the solution within the realm of your conscious mind, apply the answer and continue to move forward into your future. If you do not have the "answer," go to step two.

Step Two: Give thanks for the "experience." Ask for wisdom to learn and grow from the "experience" at hand. The healing energy this sets in motion will accomplish three things which will nourish your Soul Development.

■ It will disallow the "experience" from controlling you emotionally.

■ It will disallow the "experience" from repeating itself in your lives.

■ It will connect the conscious thought to the Spiritual Mind.

In this chapter the main focus will be the people with whom we chose to reincarnate. These people, chosen by our Soul Mind during the Review Before Return Process, provide some of the rudiments á propos to our Soul Growth Development.

THE CHOICES WE MAKE

When I conduct a Meditation Seminar, I always remind attendees that we choose our parents, we choose our gender, and we choose our race. I also say that we "sign up" for certain challenges (experiences) that provide some of the elements of our Soul Growth Development as well.

In my seminars it is not unusual for doctors, psychiatrists or psychologists to attend. During a recent seminar, I made my usual statement concerning choices as to parents, gender, and race. I noticed a man in the back of the class shaking his head vigorously from side to side, looking very perplexed. I stopped to inquire about his obvious discomfort with my statement. The man, a local psychologist, replied that he liked everything I was saying up until the statement about choosing our parents.

He went on to say there was no way in Hell that he would have done that to himself. My answer to him was simple. "Of course not consciously. But Spiritually, yes!" I reminded him that if we knew (consciously) the potential pain between point A and point B, we would not make the trip.

We do indeed re-enter the earth "experience" for a purpose. That purpose is to re-balance our Souls. The basics for this re-balancing are Soul-Self Responsibility choices. These are the people and the "experiences" our Spirit chooses before re-entry. These choices represent an individualized (Soul-Self Responsibility) expression of a Soul-to-Soul Resuscitation.

Soul-to-Soul Resuscitation choices are Bi-Liable. Each person is held accountable for his or her current-life contributions to the relationship. Our responsibility is to do what is Spiritual. So too are those we encounter in each life held liable.

Accordingly, the individuals with whom we have chosen to reincarnate in a particular life cannot control our subsequent incarnations. Each Soul must forgive and give thanks for the present-life Soul-to-Soul Resuscitation. Soul-Self Responsibility is the key to the current life Resuscitation.

During the Review Before Return process our Soul Mind (Spirit) assesses the possibilities for our return. First, the assessment is made regarding the available people. Second, the assessment is made regarding the "experiences" in accordance with our Soul Growth Issues (implying Past Lives, karma) and this-life choice. To clarify: If your Spirit chose a black family in southern Africa as opposed to a Jewish family in New York, the "experiences" encountered during that particular choice, more likely than not, would be much different. The current-life challenges (experiences) represent issues from our Past Lives in which we responded *emotionally* rather than *Spiritually*.

TWO ASSESSMENT PROCESSES

No matter the choices, similarities in our current-life challenges (experiences) may occur. However, the similarities for purpose of our discussion are too speculative to enumerate.

In accordance with the substance of this chapter, I would like to reiterate that I believe that our lives pass before us on two different and independent occasions. One is during the Near-Death Experiences that we have all heard about.

The other is what I have referred to as the Review Before Return Process.

During each occurrence we appraise our lives. The appraisals are similar as well as dissimilar. For the Near-Death Experience, we appraise our lives based on how we have lived and the resulting Growth or Non-Growth that our Soul has achieved. The Near-Death appraisal, if you will, is usually tied to an earth departure for the Soul. For the Review Before Return Process, we appraise our lives based on opportunities for reincarnation that have the potential to provide Soul Growth Development opportunities in the areas for which we still have an imbalance. The Review Before Return Process is usually based on the re-entry to earth for a Soul.

HOW FREEWILL HELPS US
TO REBALANCE OUR SOULS

The process of re-balancing our Soul is continual, whether we are departing or arriving this earth. There are, however, a few essential facts available to assist you with your effort in re-balancing your Soul.

> 1. First and foremost, we are given Freewill. This is the most powerful gift bestowed on humankind by God.
> 2. Second, Freewill is the spark that ignites the power of our Thoughts, our Words and our Deeds. Our Thoughts, Words and Deeds are the very fountain on which our future rests. We have a responsibility to our Soul Development to consciously monitor these three segments of our existence daily.
> 3. And finally, like begets like. This concept is crucial and simple: Change your thoughts, and you change your life. Your life can be better than your attitude, but you have to change it first!

Realizing that it begins and ends with our thoughts is such a simple concept, yet many strive to make it more complex. Someone said to me not long ago that he wanted to change his life, but it was so difficult. The truth of the matter is that it is no more difficult to change your life than it is to change your thoughts. Your life will chase after your thoughts; however, your thoughts will not chase you down the street! If we say we can't change, then indeed we will not! We have verbalized a self-acceptable excuse by making such a statement.

Listen to what you say. There is an old saying that the road to hell is paved with good intentions. I think we can add self-acceptable excuses to that as well. Saying that it is so hard to change anything is a good excuse for doing nothing, right? THINK about it. . . .

The realization that there is power in our thoughts, power in our words, and power in our deeds provides a phenomenal inspiration. However, this power can be expressed in a positive or negative way. When an "experience" is raging in our life and we whine, moan and groan about all that is going on, we are in essence, embracing a negative energy. As a consequence of this behavior, a negative vibration begins to envelop our lives, attracting people and events that are negative as well.

We must think, speak, and act in such a manner as not to allow an "experience" to consume us through our emotional, conscious mind. We must remind ourselves to:

1. Analyze: Do we have the answer consciously? If not,
2. Give thanks for the "Experience," and ask for wisdom to learn and grow.

It can hardly be more simple than that. Fix it if you can (consciously) and move forward into your future. Give thanks for it if you do not have the resolve in your conscious data bank. That simply means you are looking directly at either a Soul Growth Issue or Soul Grief Choice. You are not *expected* to have the answer consciously for that which your Spirit (Soul Mind) chose during your Review Before Return Process.

ISSUES, CHOICES, AND THE PEOPLE IN OUR LIVES

A Soul Growth Issue or a Soul Grief Choice can be a person, a circumstance or an issue that you chose to "experience" for your Soul Development. Soul Growth Issues imply karma and are reflective of our Past Lives. Soul Grief Choices are not tied to our Past Lives, nor do they imply karma. The latter implies God's love expressed on the earth-plane by way of our Soul's choice during The Review Before Return Process.

Our parents can be a part of our Soul Growth Issues, or Soul Grief Choices. In fact, all of our family, our friends, co-workers and even the people we encounter in the supermarket, on the freeway, or in the hospital are part of our Soul Growth Issues or Soul Grief Choices. These people are part of the varied "experiences" we encounter for our Soul-to-Soul Resuscitation.

In each life experience we encounter people who cause us to recoil immediately as they approach. They can evoke emotions of anger, frustration or anxious feelings that we do not like and cannot explain. These are old enemies (a Soul Imbalance) that we are encountering from a previous life.

Then there are those we encounter for whom we immediately feel intense feelings of love and compassion and extreme attractions.

These are our friends and lovers (Soul Harmonies) from our past lives.

It is not unusual for an old enemy, or a Soul Balance requirement, to appear in the structure of our families. This placement makes certain that we cannot reject the significance of the encounter in the present life as it pertains to our Soul Development. To be sure, we must work something out with such persons when their placement in our life is through family ties.

Conversely, sometimes an old enemy or Soul Balance requirement of the past will cross our pathway again, outside of kinship. These encounters are usually less significant to our Soul Development. Such encounters usually affect us through our emotions, often with little else predominating the encounter except the emotional "experience." The substance of this Soul-to-Soul Resuscitation grapples with overcoming the emotional control.

However, kinship usually denotes a Soul Growth Issues or Soul Grief Choice, paramount to our very connection with our Spirit (Soul Mind). It is through our Soul-to- Soul Resuscitation that this connection becomes significant to our Soul Development.

This process (conscious) is responsive to our thoughts, our words and our deeds. Most of us can recall a difficult "experience" with a family member. In some "experiences" the difficulty can persist throughout the tenure of the earth-life connection.

Keeping a distance, geographically and emotionally, can be the best approach. However, there still remains that void we feel when our family connections are fractured. Many will decry their plight in life while focusing totally on family ties as the reason for their failures. "If only they had better show-me's or go-by's."

They could have done much better with a little encouragement." Herein lies the substance for an Illusion.

It can seem exasperating and impossible at times to resolve these types of encounters connected with the current-life Soul-to-Soul Resuscitation. However, keep in mind, *it is not about blame, it is about growth*. Therefore, all is not lost as it pertains to our Soul Development.

HOW FAITH WORKS

We can advance Spiritually if we remember to pray daily and ask God to bring about a change between ourselves and the person in question that would make for a more harmonious relationship, for everyone involved.

We are thus providing the energy for our Soul Development. When this prayer has been said, leave it alone! Do not sit and watch for the change in the other person. The change may need to occur, and can be occurring, within you!

Keep in mind, as well, that you have no less than an ability to co-create your future along with God each day. To accomplish this, however, you will find it helpful to focus on the following Spiritual truths:

1. God is Love
2. There are only two emotions in the universe. Love and Fear.
3. If what you are thinking, speaking or doing does not make you feel LOVELY, it is FEAR-based.
4. Like begets like. Don't get hung up on this. It is simple. In the sum and substance of this truth, if you think, speak, or act in a negative way, you will look up and see negative people as well as negative events being attracted into your life.
5. It is not our needs, wants, or desires that will bring God's response. It is our Faith.
6. The Spirit is All-Knowing! The Conscious Mind is limited to what it has learned or been taught in any given life.

FAITH VS. FEAR

I often give an acronym to assist people in dealing with fear. It is as follows:

F (Faith)
E (Expressed)
A (Above)
R (Rationale)

To abolish fear, you must display Faith! It is not complicated. Do not make it so. Do not do battle with the "rationale!" Remember the previous discussion about Soul Growth Issues and Soul Grief Choices? Once you determine the circumstance at hand has been chosen by your Soul Mind, you must simply give thanks for the "experience," ask for wisdom to learn and grow and move ahead into your future. This serves to enhance your Soul-to-Soul Resuscitation efforts.

In doing so, you express by your very actions that you are moving ahead in Faith! No, you do not consciously have the answer for the circumstance that confronts you at the time. Your Spirit (Soul Mind) chose the "experience." You will understand only after you have embraced the circumstance and given thanks.

It is at that point your conscious thought is connected with you Spirit Mind. You no longer see through a glass darkly. . .

PATTERNS OF ENERGY

If we do our part by exercising our Free Will to monitor our thoughts, our words and our deeds, we can truly become a co-creator along with God each day as it pertains to our Soul Development. If indeed it is true that like begets like, what are the possibilities with this power we possess?

When our Spirit chooses to reincarnate, we must experience certain "Patterns of Energy." To be sure, some of these patterns are astrological influences at the time of our re-entry to earth. Patterns of Energy also are brought into our Spirit choice by way of the people with whom we choose to reincarnate as well. These people are part of our Soul-to-Soul Resuscitation.

The Spirit gave me an awareness that I often like to share:
- We all grow up physically in our teens. We go through puberty then.
- We begin to grow mentally when we are in our twenties. We usually complete our education during this phase of our lives and make a commitment to work as well as to a personal relationship.
- We begin to grow emotionally in our thirties. Our

temperament and personality are honed during this period. It is at this point the realization process of needs that are "our"-related begin to emerge. What are "our" needs? What are "our" wants? What are "our" beliefs? This is quite necessary in preparing for our forties.

● For the most part, we do not begin to grow Spiritually until we reach our forties. As a rule, it takes the human psyche a period of forty-plus years to realize that we are not committing a blasphemous act just because we have a different view than what we have been taught. Many times Freewill is not emphasized in our earlier formative years. As a matter of fact, Freewill is given little attention until we individually begin to question our lives in terms of "our" beliefs, "our" wants, and "our" needs.

Logically, it may seem something of a dichotomy to choose parents with whose beliefs we may sharply conflict in our adulthood. However, remember we did not choose the parental influence logically. We chose it Spiritually. In addition our Soul-Mind may have had assorted reasons for choosing to come through a particular environment.

As an example, some people possess tremendous talents (Past Lives Knowledge), which they have learned and accumulated in their previous incarnations. These can be distinct in terms of music, art, speaking, teaching, inventive aptitude, etc. Some of the most talented Souls in the universe have chosen to incarnate into families whose influence upon them would never allow such talents to be expressed. Conversely, some very talented Souls have been encouraged by their families to excel in areas where obvious talents exist.

The expression of talents is always tied to need in relationship to our Soul Development. In other words, do we "need" to be a musician in this particular life to accomplish Soul Growth?

Does our current-life Soul-to-Soul Resuscitation contract specify music?

From a personal perspective, I believe we know at a very early age the pathway that we are to follow in our life. I always knew as a child that I wanted to and was destined to help people. This knowing with me was innate. Helping people would provide the basis of my current-life Soul-to-Soul Resuscitation.

I believe in my most inner being that we came into this experience (life) with all the answers contained within our Higher Selves. We are simply here in this life attempting to learn to blend the ego with the Spirit. Every nuance of every individual must, at last, become blended with the Spirit.

BRINGING THE SPIRIT
OUT OF THE SHADOWS

The many activities that we must become associated with while in physical form tend to overshadow the Spiritual part of our lives if we are not ever-mindful of our need for Spiritual balance.

The overshadowing of this balance can occur from our association with parents, organized dogma, friends, work environment, academia, etc. It is very important to remember to set aside a time for prayer, and meditation each day. I often tell people to do nothing until they check with their Spirit first. The balance that is necessary in each and every one of our lives must be found through our own efforts to tap into that All-Knowing energy that is often referred to as our Spirit or Soul Mind.

When we seek this balance, challenges become growing

experiences and we comprehend the balance is not external, but within. It is essential for our Soul Development that we remember that we are Mind, Body, and Spirit. All three in one. However, the Spirit will not impose a direction on our lives. By our Freewill approach, we must make the effort for the connection with our Spirit Mind. It is through our Freewill efforts that the five senses are closed down externally (consciously) and made available for connection of the Spirit with the physical form.

There are patterns of energy that we go through in our lives, where it is to our advantage to step aside mentally and physically and invite our Spirit to take the lead. This of course happens when we do not have the answer within our conscious data bank to resolve the challenges (experiences) at hand. We must remind ourselves, however, not to default to a place of worry and fear.

Doing so embraces a negative energy and begins to create a negative vibration that surrounds our very lives. Remember, life can be better than your attitude, but you must change it first! It is simple. Like begets like. So, as long as we hold onto the negative, we are attracting the same in response. It is also important to remember you have the ability, with Freewill, to give yourself permission to be who and what you are. This ability has the capacity to eradicate the guilt from your life, as beliefs that are different from those of your parents become your focus.

It is not the beliefs that come from the parental influences in your life that are important. It is the "experience" of these beliefs that can provide your Soul Growth.

In other words, you don't have to consciously understand or like your family or the beliefs they hold. You just have to have the "experience."

Remember, that which you cannot figure out consciously was indeed chosen by your Soul Mind exclusively for your

Soul Development. Like is conscious. Love is Spiritual. Therefore, consciously (in person) you do not have to be around family you do not like.

Often the limiting beliefs of our family members can provide the "behind-the-scenes" parameters that hold our Soul in a pattern of what we may consider an ineffectual expression. We will not become the concert pianist. We will not become the commercial artist. Such is the stuff of Soul-to-Soul Resuscitations.

An outcome like these can be important to our ultimate Soul Development.

When you become an adult, do not continue to blame your parents for what you have not become. To do so shows you are living in the past. To do so voids the potential of the Soul-to-Soul Resuscitation provided by these encounters.

To do so also speaks volumes about the absence of Freewill operating in your life. To do so speaks to the failure on your part to take responsibility of your **thoughts, words and deeds,** which has the power to bring change into your life. We cannot grow Spiritually unless we are continually looking and moving ahead. *The past is only an "experience," not a way of life, unless you make it so.*

CHAPTER

8

POURING OUT FROM WITHIN: CONNECTING WITH YOUR SPIRIT

The conscious thought process frequently becomes the dungeon wherein our lives are held captive. The gate-keepers, Fear and Despair, incessantly scoff at our sanity, while they push us deeper and deeper into the cold and damp darkness. Feelings of desolation begin to resonate in the very vibration, the ethereal energy that encompasses our lives in the physical form. Searching frantically through the vast expanse of all that we know consciously, we begin to comprehend the answer we have been seeking is not external, but within.

It is especially important in the busy modern world that we remind ourselves (thought energy) daily that we are indeed physical, mental, *and* spiritual. ALL THREE in ONE! Many of us have been conditioned over the years by parents, peers, academia, and organized dogma that we must "figure things out," "be a winner," "do not give up," etc.—all consciously-directed clichés. The list of platitudes is endless.

A WELL OF SPIRITUAL KNOWLEDGE

However, it is vitally important for our Soul Development that we pause and take the time to re-remember that we have direct access to an unbelievable All-Knowing, Healing, Soul-Renewing Source of Information! Incredibly, the *Supernatural design* of the Universe has placed this extraordinary reservoir of information WITHIN each and every individual on the planet.

This reservoir is our Soul Mind, Spirit Mind, Higher Self—whatever label you choose is subjectively appropriate.

Unfortunately, this phenomenal Source of Knowledge has been greatly diminished and virtually LOST over the past few thousand years.

Concept upon concept, layer upon layer, this loss has progressively occurred over time. Essentially because of the influence of various dogmas and of the scientific community, the connection with our Higher Selves has been substantially eroded.

One segment of the population mandates that we must believe and live a certain way or suffer unimaginable consequences! Another segment of society tells us that we cannot do so unless it can be proven under certain predetermined and controlled scientific conditions.

This Internal Reservoir of Knowledge contains information that pertains to our Past Lives as well as our Present Lives. A great deal of insight that is continually being collected relates to our Future. This Reservoir can only be accessed by way of prayer and meditation. Until we, by our Freewill approach, make the effort to tap into this Reservoir, it will remain for the most part, in an inoperative state.

Occasionally we may experience flashes, insights, feelings, intuitive responses. Shaking our heads in bewilderment, we tell someone close to us that "we just knew." This sort of knowledge has been, is, and will remain available to us at all times. The flashes, insights, feelings, intuitive responses, all will continue to flow from this Reservoir of Knowledge that is found within our inner being.

The source of this well I am speaking of is at the Soul Level, The Superconscious Mind or Soul Mind.

Few of us have been conditioned to realize that the conscious mind is limited to only what it has learned or been taught in any given life. The Spirit Mind however, *that eternal well within us, is All-Knowing!*

DRAWING FROM THE WELL

How, you might ask, do we access this information? Is it difficult to tap into this incredible source of understanding? Does a person need years of training and practice to draw from this Well of Knowledge? Absolutely not! The answer is, in fact, quite simple! This *All-Knowing Source of Wisdom and Healing Power* can be easily accessed through Prayer and Meditation! Prayer is talking to God, with the result that we surround ourselves with Light and Love. Meditation is listening to God. The Superconscious Mind within us (our Soul Mind) is the very energy that connects us directly to God. *Our souls are part of the God force!* We must take the time to listen. And it is so simple!

Every human on this planet is tied together by way of the Universal Subconsciousness. In other words, we are all connected. *Whatever we do one to another, we do to ourselves!* This Universal Subconsciousness is the human equivalent to the Internet! What a wealth of information we have within easy reach! There is, in actuality, no problem that we cannot explicate through this Spiritual Internet!

I have been teaching meditation for many years. As a result of my comprehensive involvement, I have found that many methods being taught are made far too difficult. It is important to keep in mind one simple truth about all aspects of the Spirit. *Simplicity!* That which would establish too much rigidity and control cannot be of the Spirit It must, by this very fact, be of Man!

In my opinion, when people make meditation difficult, it is for purpose of control. Spirituality is subjective, not objective. Therefore, aside from the basics, it is important to keep in mind that there are as many ways to meditate as there as people on the planet.

MEDITATION: A FEW PLAIN FACTS

I would like to share a few of these basics that I have found most helpful personally. I have also found these same tenets to be beneficial to the thousands that I have taught over the years. Once you have learned the basics, you are on your own, so to speak. When you first begin, you can sit, lie down, listen to music, burn incense, or burn candles--whatever you deem necessary and appropriate during your earliest efforts to meditate. Never allow anyone to say THIS is the only way to meditate. *But do keep in mind though that the burning of candles or incense, listening to music, chanting a mantra, all keep you on the conscious level. In our effort to access our higher selves, it is the conscious mind that we must set aside.*

For those who are just beginning the process of meditation, the aforementioned processes of music, candles and incense can be a great help. But as one becomes more experienced in drawing from the Well within, all external (conscious) efforts will be effortlessly set aside.

During a break in a seminar I taught not long ago, a lady approached me and said she had been taking a particular type of meditation for thirty years. (It serves no purpose to reveal the name of this system; suffice it to say that the method is very well known.) My first response to her was *Why?* Hoping that she would understand the levity of my next question, I asked her, with a smile, if she was a slow learner. Her reply was "Oh, no, They just keep you coming back."

It is not necessary to have years of training to tap into the energy that has always been, and will continue to be, a part of you. It is just a matter of knowing how! You simply need to re-remember how to "dial into" this source.

I have taught a beginning and an advanced meditation for several years. The beginning class gives you all the tools you need to access the Higher Power that YOU carry around with you everywhere you go! The advanced class teaches you how to cleanse and balance the Seven Spiritual Centers (Chakras).

We can hold a lot of physical, mental and Spiritual dis-ease in these centers. Clearing these Spiritual centers is essential in our continued Soul Development! It is my sincere belief that after learning the methodology presented in these two seminars, one need search no further for the way to communicate with the Higher Self. Let me explain.

USING CONSCIOUS FREEWILL
TO CONTACT THE SOUL

Most would agree that we function, on an everyday conscious level, through the central nervous system. The central nervous system consists of portions of the brain, the spinal cord, the musculoskeletal system and the five senses. Most would also agree that we can affect or control this assemblage by input from our conscious minds. Freewill! As an example, we can choose to walk, talk, smell or touch whenever we want. But, let us not forget another system that is part of our lives. Called the *autonomic nervous system*, it consists of the sympathetic/parasympathetic system, the organs and the glands (including the endocrine glands, which work with the Spiritual Centers, the chakras) of our physical bodies.

The Subconscious basically controls this system. The Subconscious and the Soul (Superconscious Mind) join in regulating temperature, chemistry, sustenance, heartbeat, breathing, and digestion while responding to the requirements of the outer system. Any time that we, by our conscious will, start to affect any or all of our five senses, we are in essence automatically sending a message to our Superconscious Mind, Soul Mind, Spirit Mind, Higher Selves (whatever label you choose) that we want input from a higher source. By this very action, we are willing to set aside our outer, conscious selves and make the effort to activate our Soul, (Superconscious Mind). So, as you can readily see, when we sit down and diminish our sense perception by the conscious cessation of our five senses—close your eyes, stop touching, stop listening, stop smelling and tasting—we begin to activate our Soul. How simple!

The Subconscious and the Soul (Superconscious Mind) regulate our breathing by way of the autonomic system. When we begin by our Freewill to regulate the breathing, the Soul and the Subconscious Mind becomes vigilant. This simple action will lead from our outer, conscious selves to our inner All-Knowing, Healing Selves and ultimately to an altered state of consciousness.

HOW TO START THE PROCESS

To activate this All-Knowing Healing Energy, *your Soul,* do the following: Sit down in a private place, where you will not be disturbed. Close your eyes and begin to take in a few deep breathes. Breathe in deeply through the nostrils, hold it for a few seconds and then exhale through the mouth and hold the exhale for a few seconds.

Ten to twelve deep breaths will suffice to realign the Spiritual Energy (the Soul Energy) within the physical form.

This is the initial point at which you can begin to communicate with your "Higher Self." In essence this simple procedure has given you the *dial tone* to speak to your "Higher Self"—that All-Knowing, Healing Energy that we all possess!

Your Soul Mind can communicate with the physical form only through the five senses.

This procedure closes down the five senses from external (conscious) use, providing the connection between the Spiritual and the physical. Keep in mind that, while I suggest you begin your day this way, this method will work at any time during the day as well.

Each time I teach a meditation class, I write a phrase on the board for the class to see as they enter the room. It is as follows:

Be   Still
(Inhale) (Exhale)

And Know God
(Inhale) (Exhale)

Many people have said to me that they cannot quiet their conscious minds so that they can meditate. Not true! We have Free Will! Therefore, we have the ability to co-create with God that which we want. If we want to meditate, then indeed we can. It is just the matter of taking the initiative by way of our Freewill, our *power spark*, to ignite this process.

I usually begin each meditation class with a similar statement. I ask the class participants to sit up straight, with both feet on the floor, palms turned up on their laps and eyes closed.

Then I say the word *Be* (instructing the class to inhale deeply through their nostrils and hold it); then I say the word *Still* (instructing the class to exhale deeply through their mouths and hold it), and then continue with the words *And Know* and *God*, with the accompanying breathing instructions. Prior to this exercise, I usually ask the class to note their "energy" level. Then after completion of the exercise I ask, by a show of hands, how many felt this breathing exercise was beneficial to them. I also ask how many felt that their energy level changed?

Without exception, 99.99 percent of the class feels more centered, relaxed, peaceful, and in tune.

WHEN MEDITATION HELPS: A PRACTICAL EXAMPLE

There have been many occasions when I simply had no answer to a particular challenge that was going on in my life at the time. I now know and understand that these challenges are actually "Soul Growth Issues" or "Soul Grief Choices." When we have analyzed the possibilities for a solution from our conscious minds without resolution, we have come face-to-face with one of our "Soul Growth Issues" or "Soul Grief Choices." It is at this very point that we should turn to our Soul Mind (Superconscious Mind).

Not long ago such a challenge manifested itself in my conscious mind. To summarize, I will simply say I switched office leases with a client. He needed a larger space (which I had), and I needed a smaller space (which he had). I was closing down a store and moving my office when this "perfect" (so I thought) solution presented itself.

Less than a week after making the change, I realized that I had made a terrible mistake. I could hear conversations, verbatim, from the offices on either side of mine.

To further complicate matters, two women in one of the offices had delivered babies within a week of one another and were bringing them to work daily to breast-feed. When I complained about the noise, I was informed by one of the women that I should have thought of that before I moved in. I quickly learned from many of the other tenants that the noise problem in the complex was an old issue, and nothing would ever be done about it.

The frustration and anger I felt was beyond explanation. I had just signed a two-year lease. One day while sitting in my office, taking in a few deep breathes, asking God why had this been allowed to transpire in my life, a miracle began to unfold. I had just closed my eyes to do my deep breathing exercise when there was a knock on my office door. My assistant said a woman I should speak with was in the outer office.

In this particular complex, a covered walkway passes by the door of each office suite. My assistant had noticed the woman walking by our door, turning around and coming back on several occasions. Thinking that she might be a client looking for me, my assistant went out and asked the lady if she needed any help. She simply said, "No, I am looking for office space and for some reason I keep being drawn back to this door." My assistant told her to please come in and speak with me.

The woman was a massage therapist. When I told her that I had to move because of the noise factor, she stated that she did not think that she would be as sensitive to the noise level as I was and would be willing to talk about taking over my lease. You cannot imagine my delight. I do believe that the angels brought this person to my very door.

I did not have the conscious answer to this circumstance, but my Soul Mind (Superconscious Mind) did. What more could I want? All I needed to re-learn was to follow (rely on) the Spirit, in ALL things, instead of depending on my conscious mind. In my conscious frustration I had forgotten this priceless knowledge. Did this experience serve to build my faith? You bet! Over and over I have been reminded how the Spirit will lead, IF we are willing to follow.

OVER AND OVER AGAIN I AM REMINDED: *The conscious mind is limited to what it has learned or been taught. The Soul Mind is All-Knowing.*

CHAPTER

9

BREAKING OUR STRAWS

I t is my belief that the Ten Commandments are Divine. These "rules," from a Spiritual Perspective, were given as a "guide" by which to conduct our lives during our visit to this planet. Consequently, I feel that no other directives are relevant to our Soul Development. Although I was skeptical for a while, I now do believe these Ten Laws are Divine. After all, if you ask whether these Laws would apply to a Muslim, Hindu, Buddhist, Catholic, Protestant, Jewish or Native American person, the answer unequivocally would be YES! If you ask whether these Laws would apply to a White person, a Black person, a German, Italian, Irish, Indian, an Arab, or anyone else, the answer unequivocally, would be YES!

I hope that what the Spirit has shared with me, contained within this book, will serve to prompt all the readers of this book to adhere more in their future to that which is Spiritual, rather than to that which is religious. Perhaps then, one day the two can become synonymous.

Spirituality implies acceptance of everyone, regardless of race, creed, or color.

Spirituality implies Freewill. *Anything that separates, segregates, or sets itself apart cannot be of God.*

Anything that abolishes Freewill is not of God. It is of man, for purpose of control. *Accordingly, laws dictated by organized dogma, apart from The Ten Commandments, set aside Freewill.*

Historically, laws of dogma that do not resonate with The Commandments have been harsh as well as self-serving. As an example: Women today are still suppressed in most religious beliefs. Segmenting of the population by race, creed, or color as well as lifestyle still flourishes in many religious communities today. Abortion is condemned by zealots everywhere.

It would seem simple enough to use these Commandments as a barometer in all religious beliefs. After all, the seven major religions—Muslim, Hindu, Buddhist, Catholic, Protestant, Jewish and Native American—ALL possess credos that are very similar to the Ten Commandments. *It is the departure from these Laws that accommodates the hate that exists in our world today.*

While I do not discourage people from attending the place of worship of their choice, I surely do discourage anyone from implying that if you do not believe as they believe, then you are wrong. Personally, I believe if we follow any religious dogma that does not adhere to The Ten Commandments, we are following someone's ego.

THE TEN UNIVERSAL LAWS

Many years ago, I set out to determine if indeed The Ten Commandments harmonized with the major religious belief systems around the world.

If The Ten Commandments were from a Divine source, wasn't it safe to conjecture, then, that they would display a congruent resonance with all major belief systems? A common thread, if you will?

These of course were the Ten Laws allegedly given to Moses by God and recorded on the stone tablet. However, I was always somewhat dubious about the story of Moses and the Ten Commandments.

This story seemed incredible to me, since it is commonly known that Moses was raised by the Egyptians. We also know that the Egyptians had an apparatus in which they housed their sacred records, which bore extreme similarities to the one that Moses supposedly said God told him to prepare as a repository for the Ten Commandments. Moreover, I knew from my years of study that much of what is contained in the Biblical text was not written down until forty to one hundred years, or more, after the occurrences it records.

The seven translations of this material that led to what is now known as the King James Bible further piqued my curiosity about The Ten Laws' efficacy.

Armed with this understanding I decided to appraise the seven major religious belief systems in an effort to determine their resonance with the Ten Commandments.

The ones that I assessed were Muslim, Hindu, Buddhist, Catholic, Protestant, Jewish and Native American. I was very pleased to discover that each of these belief systems does indeed possess a credo that is very similar to the Ten Commandments. They correspond so well, you can almost check them off one by one. It was also interesting to note that each of these belief systems chronicled a catastrophe much like the Biblical account of the great flood.

This led me to the realization that we are not so far apart in the world as it pertains to the essence of our religious beliefs. However, we remain worlds apart in our judgments.

Today, the congruence is found only in the basic tenets of each belief. There it ends.

FEAR, GUILT, AND RELIGIOUS DOGMA

In terms of the Ten Commandments, our judgments consist of all of the number 11's, 12's, and so on. Any time religious dogma states that we should do thus-and-so, we have a responsibility to our very Soul Development to stop and ask ourselves, which of the Ten Commandants says this?

From a secular perspective, we must abide by city, state and federal laws that help to govern our day-to-day lives. These laws provide the basis that allows us to learn to live together in close proximity.

From a Spiritual perspective, we are not here to follow Man's law (organized dogma). Rather, I believe, we are here to follow God's law, The Ten Commandments.

"THE BIGGEST SINNER ON THE PLANET"

People frequently condemn themselves for behavior that they have been taught to believe is a "sin!" However, we must remember, Spirituality requires unlearning Self-judgment. Let me share a couple of stories with you.

A few years ago I was visiting with a client who teaches at a local university when she told me that she felt like the biggest sinner on the planet. When I inquired as to why she would make such a statement, she told me "I have been saying the "f" word all week at work." My response was simply to ask, "What else?" It was obvious that she was extremely troubled as she continued to tell me that she grew up affiliated with a religious belief system that had taught her that if she said ugly words, she was a sinner and was going to hell.

I assured my client that she had been misinformed. Very rarely have I observed a more quizzical look on a person's face than when I made that statement to her. It was obvious that my client was anxious to hear something that had the potential to assist her in dealing with her emotional and mental pain.

I continued by asking her, "Which of the Ten Commandments says "thou shall not say the "f" word?" Her response was, "You know, none of them says that!"

Of course I knew that none of the Ten Commandments says that. I continued our session by assuring her that she had not sinned at all. She had just been very human. Maybe she was somewhat socially unacceptable around the campus that week, but sin was not involved.

She stared at me intently (I could tell the wheels were turning in her conscious mind) and then said, "F___, I sure feel better!" She stood up, thanked me profusely, and left my office. The next morning when I came into the office, a young lady who works for me part-time told me there was a message in voice mail that she didn't not know how to handle. (No, it is not what you are thinking!) I told her I would take care of it. When I dialed into voice mail, a woman's voice said, "Thirty-nine and counting" and then hung up.

I recognized the professor's voice and called her at the university. I asked her what was thirty-nine and counting? My client was so excited she could hardly talk. She told me that after she left my office, she could not get out of her head my question about which of the Ten Commandments said she could not say the "f" word.

Using the Ten Commandments as a reference point, she began to recount all of the many things about which she had been made to feel guilty, fearful or controlled. Tracing these issues back to their origin, my client did not take long to realize that these issues were, for the most part, based on the religious belief she had experienced earlier in life.

What a wonderful revelation! Realizing that 95 percent or more of her fear, guilt and control issues were the progeny of religious belief, made the healing effort so much easier! Each fear, each guilt and each control issue could simply be held up against the backdrop of the Ten Commandments. Congruity would serve as the common thread. Each time she thought of an issue that was attached to fear, guilt or control, she would stop and ask herself, "Which one of the Ten Commandments says this?"

My client said using this approach had enabled her to erase thirty-nine of those old messages in a very short time, for which she was infinitely grateful. The next time I saw my friend, it was more than apparent she had accomplished Spiritual freedom! It was very clear that she had dealt with the past, healed it, and was now anxiously looking forward to her Spiritual future!

ORGANIZED DOGMA VS. TRUE SPIRITUALITY

As I continue to observe the world in association with organized dogma, I am sorely disappointed. As dogmatic religions manifest themselves today, they appear to have a foundation that is, in fact, based on fear, guilt and control.

Let me explain. Quite often I have noticed people adhering to religious dogma and ignoring God's ten laws. For example, why do people who call themselves religious and Christians continue to kill one another in Ireland? Clearly, one of the Ten Commandments admonishes us not to kill!

Why do the Christians, Jews and Muslims relentlessly persevere in the fighting and killing of one another in the Middle East over the West Bank, the East Bank, and an old piece of a wall or the Gaza Strip? Why are we not focusing on God instead of material things? God is love. Warring over material possessions is not in keeping with THIS love!

Why do the Jews persist in the killing to take back The Dome of The Rock? Why do the Muslims persist in the killing to keep The Dome of The Rock? Each of their religions claims the space as Holy unto itself. So, we must ask: How many have died on each side of this issue since both parties decided that this space is sacred unto them?

The question could easily be what Italian, what German, or what Gypsy wrote these things. In every conflict, each side claims it is not they that want to continue the fighting and killing—it is the other side. What God of which Universe would say to either side, "Yeah, Jews, kill those Muslims?" Or "Yeah, Muslims, kill those Jews?" What God of which Universe would have the world support selfishness for any ethnic group?

Why do the Serbs persist in trying to keep the practice of genocide alive in Yugoslavia? They do call themselves religious. Were they not the very ones who drove the Jewish people out of that area in World War II? So, do they think that only "their kind" has a right to be in that area? Are we not told to "love our neighbor as ourselves"?

Why do many of the religious belief systems of today possess such great material wealth (money, artworks, investments, etc.) and sit idly by while people in their own communities or around the world starve to death? We need to remember how the churches obtained this wealth. From the communities! Then why do we look out in our communities and see the homeless, with nowhere to go?

Arizona's urban Maricopa County, where I live, manages to support twenty-one synagogues, seven mosques, and enough Christian churches to fill *eighteen pages* of the telephone book with fine-print listings. Yet in the same community, one out of four children goes to bed hungry every night.

Why?

How can we say we know God when our material treasures take precedence over a Soul in need? Where is our focus?

Should material possessions and financial wealth become more prominent in our religious belief systems, as it seems they have, than the effort to help those in need?

Is it not painfully obvious that if we don't give when we have a dollar, we will not give when we have millions? Why are the great religious storehouses of the world hoarding such incalculable material wealth? Is indeed a statue, a painting, a certificate of deposit or any other measure of material wealth Spiritually more significant than helping the frail mothers we see reflected in the media, holding onto children that are little more than skin stretched over a skeleton?

Can it be that we have forgotten that growing Spiritually IS caring about others?

"THE POOR ARE ALWAYS AMONG US"

A few years ago I visited Rome with a friend of mine. Of course we went to the Vatican. While observing all the artwork, which includes famous paintings and statuary, I was struck by the veneration one feels, viewing such splendor.

I saw a priest who was obviously assigned to the Vatican and began a conversation with him. My interest was not so much in the magnificence of the Vatican's collection, but rather in when and where the church had changed its focus.

I asked the priest why the church was so focused on material things: things that man had created and which were supposedly of incalculable worth. Why was the church not focused on what God had created lying right outside of their gate?

The priest said he did not understand my line of questioning. I went on to remind him that as tourist we have to pass the homeless, the sick and the hungry to come in and view the Church's great storehouse of priceless treasures. I asked him why the Church did not give these things to Mother Theresa? She would surely sell them and with the proceeds help the homeless, the sick and the hungry.

That gift would reverberate throughout eternity. I reminded him just as the Colosseum has turned to dust, so too will these great artworks one day turn to dust. I asked him when that occurred, who would benefit?

As he turned to walk away, his comment was that we would always have the poor among us. So I asked him was it all right that the church kept their priceless artwork and let the people in Ethiopia starve to death?

I followed him, asking what he believed God would say if He were present that day. "By all means keep your priceless artifacts, but do not feed those mothers or children that are starving to death in Ethiopia?"

The priest turned around and glared at me with such an intensity of reproach, I felt like a knife had been plunged into my heart. I have no doubt that if looks could kill, I would have died on the spot.

Looking around the world, it is not difficult to reach the conclusion that religion seems to separate man from God, and man from man. Is it therefore preposterous to hypothesize that it appears the Devil is getting far more mileage out of this thing called religion than God? Nothing else seems to separate the world's population more. Nothing else seems to cause so much conflict in the human experience.

THE PSYCHOLOGICAL FALLOUT FROM ORGANIZED RELIGION

Feeling fearful. Feeling guilty. Feeling controlled. These are the byproducts of man's religious laws set into motion against man, and, I believe, against God.

When considering the Ten Commandments, take note: If just the populace in the world that is connected to the seven major religious beliefs would follow these Ten Laws, consummate peace would be achieved around the world.

It is my hope as well as my prayer that we will find that the road to Spirituality does not require everyone to look alike, think alike, speak the same language, or, to embrace a particular organized dogma.

Many people feel more comfortable with a structured regimen in their approach to God. However, do you not find it curious why so often the people who choose this type of life adjudge everyone else who does not conform to their particular belief system to be lost or bound for hell?

What are we to do with Freewill? The very things that separate humans from the animals in the wild are freewill and the ability to formulate thoughts and make decisions. How have we evolved to the point of making such judgments? Could it be that the fear, guilt and control issues of organized dogma have brought us to this place?

Could it possibly be that when we feel guilty, fearful or controlled in our belief system, we assume we must pass these same feelings on to all who do not embrace the same religious constraints as we do?

Guilt by its very nature breeds dependence. If you allow a person or an organization to make you feel guilty, you have allowed that person or organization to make you feel dependent on them. The assumption consciously and subconsciously is that they have an answer you do not.

Just by the very action of accepting guilt, you have set aside your Freewill (a God-given right) and allowed someone else to take responsibility for your Soul. Just by that very action you have brought upon yourself the destructive energy of self-judgment. It is eminently important for your Soul Development that you realize self-judgment knows no equal in the universe. If brought into your life it will only resonate in discord! Are you guilty because someone else says you are?

FALLACIES OF ORGANIZED RELIGION

Is everything taught or implied by religion reliable? I do not think so. For example, everyone associated with a Christian philosophy has been taught or it has been strongly implied that the Trinity was a Divine proclamation of God. It was not.

When Constantine brought Christianity into Rome around A.D. 325, he and his cronies wanted absolute power. So, they established the figurehead the Trinity and voted on who was to be in the membership. It was a political vote! Shocked? Look it up! It is recorded history.

It is my belief that religion and politics have not improved since that date. The reason is that they both set in emotions. And emotions, which are germane to our conscious minds, are offensive to our Spirit Minds, when it comes to decision-making!

Why are we not encouraged by all religious beliefs to take the time to learn and understand more about one another's belief systems? If we call a pencil something different in France, does it do anything different from what it does in our language? Of course not! If we were encouraged to look for the common ground in each belief system, we would quickly realize that the similarities far outweigh the dissimilarities!

Spirituality, by its very essence, cannot be a competitive effort. To become more Spiritual simply means we do not judge. It means we learn about and hopefully come to understand our differences are not so vast after all, if we embrace God's laws.

A MINISTER ON THE RIGHT TRACK

A few years ago I was very privileged to have a very dear friend visit from out of state. Early one morning I arose to make a pot of coffee and prepare for my day. My friend was already up, sitting in the den and watching TV. The program my friend was watching was one that I was not accustomed to viewing.

She was watching a program on the religious channel. When I walked past the den and heard this African-American minister on television say, "We are all of one blood," it caught my attention.

My friend from Atlanta, by the way, is a woman of color. Black, African-American, whatever label you choose. . . . More than her color, more than her ethnicity, more than her being female, she is a Spiritual human being! I have known this wonderful person for more than thirty years!

I have never communicated with her based on a color. We have always communicated with each other based on our individual Spirituality.

However, I digress. The minister on television saying that we were all of one blood intrigued me. He went on to explain that if after leaving the service today he was in an accident and needed a blood transfusion, the people at the hospital would not run out in the street and look for another black person to transfuse him. They would look for a blood type!

What a wonderful analogy! I could not believe how this statement affected my life at the Soul level! How succinct this statement about humanity! How wonderful to think that there is a measurable, tangible thread that runs throughout the human race, tying us all together with such simplicity!

REMEMBERING OUR ORIGINS

How is it that we have forgotten that we are all of one blood? The scientific community recently announced that by the use of DNA it is possible to say in fact that we are "all of one blood." So, why are we fighting with ourselves?

It is sad and simply true. We continue to fight and kill one another over a belief. What has brought us to this, that a concept or belief has become more important than someone's life? Have our concepts or beliefs become more important than our very Souls?

Day after day people all over the world claim to be religious. Day after day people all over the world discriminate against their relatives, their neighbors, their fellow employee, and anyone else who does not believe the same thing they profess. Day after day people segment the population by expletives that refer to one's gender, color, race, age, weight, belief, etc.

We must not forget that differences provide the foundation for experience. How can we possibly grow if all we are exposed to in our lives is that which is just like us? We are here in human form to experience. *Experience by its very definition is the basis of acquiring knowledge, Spiritual and secular alike.*

THE RESPONSIBILITY OF FREEWILL

In our attempts to become more Spiritual we must not forget our origin. And we must not forget that our origin is our destiny!

Each life that we "experience" is a Soul's attempt to return to that God-force (total love) that we are "origin"-ally from. It is the misuse of the human expression of Freewill that has separated our Soul from that God-force.

This same Freewill is the spark that has the capacity to Co-create our future each day along with God. In our human experience we are greatly responsible for our future and to our Souls. It is our Freewill responsibility to keep our thoughts, our words and our deeds positive. These are the three segments of our human lives for which we are "Soul"-ly responsible.

Remember the concept, like begets like? If we keep our thoughts words and deeds positive, we will look up and see positive events and people, too, being attracted into our lives.

If we are to have peace in our World, we must stand up and say to people of all countries: Believe what you want. Worship as you wish. But do not kill those who believe differently than you do. When will we say to those who continue to fight and kill in the name of their religious belief that enough is enough? When will we as a nation put Spirituality ahead of money and material contracts? When will we say as a nation if you kill people with a belief different than yours, we as a Spiritual nation will boycott you?

Are we so fear-based that we believe a particular area of the world is our supply? Does it not rather imply a turning away from God, when we put material concerns ahead of Spirituality? Do we not have a responsibility as a Spiritual nation to say to our friends in the Middle East, whether Jewish, Muslim or Christian, stop the hate? Do we not have a responsibility as a Spiritual nation to say to our friends in Ireland, stop the hate?

All of the seven major religious beliefs say not to kill. What has happened that this has been forgotten? Is the price we are willing to give in exchange for a life worth it?

Our prayer and meditative efforts can change the world! It begins with us! Should we not to say to the belief systems in the world to stop constructing these "graven images" of buildings that cost millions and millions of dollars, while ignoring the homeless, the sick and the hungry in their communities and around the world?

Why do we continue to encourage religious institutions to accumulate such wealth?

Why is it necessary for any religious belief to have more in its coffers than would sustain the yearly budgetary requirements for mortgages, utilities, salaries, repair and maintenance, and the like? Should not we insist that these institutions give the monies back to the communities whence it came?

10

UNDERSTANDING
ILLUSIONS

I llusion means falseness, fallacy, deception, delusion, mirage, fantasy, and chimera.

In our attempt to explore and understand illusions in our lives, it helps to establish an anchor from which to start. This anchor must have the potential to become the reference point for all of our experiences in the investment of our Soul Development. Once this anchor is established and accepted, we will relate to it throughout our efforts of Enlightenment and Spiritual Development.

From the moment our Soul re-enters an earth life, we are subject to patterns of energy that we have chosen to experience. The make-up of these patterns is varied. For instance we may choose to re-enter the earth during a particular astrological influence.

These influences meld with the make-up of our entire being, to include our Past Lives. However, remember that even though these influences can be extreme, our Freewill supersedes planetary as well as hereditary influences! It is not the challenge that is important in any life; it is our response to it.

THE PATTERNS OF OUR LIVES

We continue to reincarnate for one of two reasons: Soul Growth Issues, which imply karma, or Soul Grief Choices, which do not involve karma but provide the mechanism by which God's Love is made manifest in the earthly plane.

Simply put, karma in this vernacular means those experiences from our Past Lives that we responded to emotionally, instead of Spiritually. This type of response chronicles a negative energy in our Past Lives Record.

Karma also has a positive side, consisting of various patterns of energy. Let's consider a couple. As one example, the abilities we designate as talents are karmic in origin learned in a Past Life. In a second example, Edgar Cayce implied that anyone who was born rich or grew rich in any life had earned it in their previous lives; this again is an example of positive Karma.

The family into which we are born will provide certain patterns of energy. The fact that we may choose to come back as a man, a woman, an African-American person, a Hispanic person, a Caucasian person, or any other designation, will prescribe certain patterns of energy. Enduring a physical illness during our life or being born handicapped also accommodates and attracts certain patterns of energy which we are to experience in our efforts of rebalancing our Souls.

Consciously, we have no way to determine the entire composition of these patterns of energies that comprise our Soul Growth Issues or Soul Grief Choices. Until we embrace and give thanks for each experience pattern for which we consciously do not have the answer, we must repeat the pattern.

The evidence of such patterns, as well as our attendance in the current life, point to what we have contracted Spiritually to experience during this sojourn.

However, an anchor or reference point is key to our Soul Development. Depending greatly on the patterns of religious belief experience that your Soul chose to experience, this can be a very complex undertaking. Considering that the administration of religion in our lives has usually been based on a foundation of fear, guilt and control, it can take years to develop your Freewill approach.

Let's consider this a little further. First of all, when you are expressing a fear-based life, the more emotional an issue is, the more acceptable it seems to be the conscious mind. Second, if you allow an individual or institution to make you feel guilty, there is a conscious as well as a subconscious pre-programmed response assumption that "they" have the answer and you do not. Third, you must learn to embrace the realization that Freewill by its very expression would abolish control.

Now, with this understanding we can better establish our anchor or reference point. In so doing, we must also evaluate that which is said to be of God. Fortunately, it is quite simple to determine that which is of God. Remember, God is LOVE. So, if something is indeed of God, it will stand the test of the following criteria:

First, it will not segment the population on the planet in any shape, form or fashion. It will have the capacity to "accommodate" every human on earth. God will not visit a particular race, creed, or color and ignore everyone that is "different" from that particular race, creed or color.

Second, it will not impede your Freewill. YOU along with the guidance of your Spirit Mind, Soul Mind, or Higher Self (whatever label you like) have the God-given right to select the pathway that you think is best for you.

Whether we can prove the validity of the Ten

Commandments or not, they are sufficient to provide the mainstay or backdrop of our reference point. These Laws meet the two above criteria.

THE ILLUSIONS OF EARTHLY LIFE

The illusions of what consists of a sin become blurred as well as confusing if we look only through the conscious eyes of the various religious teachings. However, when we hold these varied beliefs up against the backdrop of the Ten Commandments, the illusions fade away.

Sex. Sin or not? Many belief systems relegate this natural act of the human species to the category of sin, unless this or that applies. However when sex is held up against the backdrop of the Ten Commandments, it becomes simple. Do not commit adultery. Could this mean that two consenting adults who are unmarried yet engage in a sexual relationship are not sinners? Absolutely, if we embrace the Ten Commandments as our reference point! Of course this realization does not mean one should abandon the use of common sense and precautions appropriate to such a union.

However, neither sexual desire nor its fulfillment is a sin when carried out in our lives according to the Ten Commandments. Suffice it to say most of our indoctrination regarding sex has taken place during our formative years. If this indoctrination was based on a strict religious belief system, changing this pattern will result in changes on many different levels of your life.

As I have stated previously in this writing, we have a responsibility to use the Ten Commandments as a backdrop in living our lives to our fullest potential. Those dictates in religious dogma that stray from the Commandments are, sum and substance, someone's ego concocted for the express purpose of destroying our Freewill. What an Illusion!

Illusions of "Sameness" can often become embedded in

our conscious minds to such a degree that change will not occur. We support this sameness by thinking, speaking or acting in such a manner that we "feed" and therefore keep alive and active the very energy we say we want to change.

For example: "I just seem to live from paycheck to paycheck. Every time I have a few extra dollars in my pocket, something seems to happen that consumes every penny I have. The harder I try, the further behind I get." The expression of fear can be seductive. Remember what was given earlier. The more emotional the circumstance is, the more believable it is to the conscious mind.

We can become so immersed in an energy of despair that we think we cannot imagine (objectify) a way out of the suffering we are experiencing. Consider, if you will, that like begets like. Aren't we then, by our whining moaning and groaning, perpetuating the dilemma that we perceive for our lives. YES!

USING FREEWILL TO CHANGE THE ILLUSIONS

Thoughts are things. We do have POWER in our Thoughts, our Words and our Deeds! Freewill is the vehicle for this power! The "trip" you take is limited only by your "imaginings." What will you "imagine" or "image" for your future?

In my work I often encounter people who complain about their jobs or relationships. When I admonish them to make a change, the immediate response is "the fear of the UNKNOWN." What an Illusion!

What has happened that we have allowed ourselves to become so jaded (exhausted) with the assumption that change is bad? Why have we forgotten that the Spirit is All-Knowing and the conscious mind is limited to what it has learned or been taught in any given life "experience"? Since the conscious mind is a historical data base, it is impossible for this portion of our mind to discern the future. Consciously as we look ahead we are quick to proclaim our fear of the unknown! However, when we combine the conscious mind with our Soul Mind through prayer and meditation, we have the most powerful force known to humankind to choose the pathway that is in keeping with our Soul Contract.

The process of change can be simple. You can begin change by obliterating "sameness" in your living environment. Sameness in and of itself, is an illusion. Most of us are prone to keep the closet doors in our homes as well as the drawers in our furniture closed.

To help your conscious mind (Thought Power) to proclaim change, or redefine an illusion, why not begin with your environment? By exercising our Freewill, we can begin to "image" or represent our desire for change by leaving a door or drawer open (a third of the way is what I do) in each room of our house. There is no magic in this approach at all. It is simply a reminder to our "Thought Power" that change is proclaimed!

The illusion of the way things have been will begin to fade away, allowing our Spirit to expand and grow.

Each time you walk into a room and observe an open door or drawer, it will automatically trigger your new images of change. What do the images or representation of your future look like? *Rather than just imagining your future the way you want it to be, try imagining what you would be doing if your life were already that way. This, I believe, expresses our "Thought Power" in a most dynamic way.*

Bear in mind that we choose to re-enter an earth life experience for the purpose of CHANGE! We (our Spirit Mind, our Soul Mind) have chosen to reincarnate because this life experience has the potential to assist our need to rebalance our Soul.

As I stated earlier, for the most part we are back on the earth plane because we reacted to previous life experiences emotionally rather than Spiritually.

To eradicate all the imperfections that our Freewill choices of the past have produced, CHANGE is essential. It is not enough that we drift aimlessly throughout our lives, waiting for change to randomly or haphazardly occur. Change is often the design that eradicates illusions.

Our Soul can achieve the rebalancing through our Freewill choices only while in human form. The human experience is the only time the Soul is instantaneously influenced by Freewill. Keep in mind that this also includes our Past Lives as well. For the most part, we continue to return to the human life experience for the purpose of rebalancing our Souls.

In other words, our Past Lives as well as Present Life Freewill choices are the impelling forces that prompt our Soul to re-enter the earth life experience. *To continue re-entering the earth life experience without change would become extremely counterproductive to our Soul Development.*

ILLUSIONS, BLAME, AND EXCUSES

Illusions are also developed from the myriad of excuses we proclaim while doing nothing. Nevertheless, we must remember that inactivity starves the Spirit (Soul). For example, I have often heard people say that they wanted to stop smoking, but wanted to wait until they changed jobs. The current job being very stressful (emotional) becomes the affliction (illusion) in their entire energy. Everything that is inharmonious now in life has a Blame Thread tied to this one challenge. Now we have a layered illusion.

This same mind-set often is applied to an individual's life in relationship to their childhood. Frequently, people will attach a *Blame Thread* from their past, formative years to their present disappointments in adulthood. Such a mind-set (illusion) serves to attract into our lives the pageantry, people and events that keep our vibration revved up to the level of the illusion that we imprinted on at an earlier age.

Until we embrace and give thanks for these experiences, the illusions germane to our formative years will continue to infuse our adulthood.

As such, it is important to understand that the family experiences (illusions) that were chosen during the Review before Return Process serve to keep the parameters around the contract you made for the present life. Unless you embrace your past, it is impossible to understand your Soul Contract in any given life expression. It is not about blame; it is about Growth!

FREEING OURSELVES THROUGH CHANGE

Past Lives experiences reflect into our future as Soul Growth Issues (illusions from our past) expressed through contact with the patterns of energy into which we reincarnate.

Further, until we clear (heal) the energy patterns with those that we chose to reincarnate in any life, repetition of sameness will continue in subsequent life expressions. Remember it is not the ending of a relationship (change) that is important! It is how we bring the relationship to the point of change that will determine our Soul Development!

As stated in a previous chapter, our earth life experiences are BI-liable. This means that once you have given thanks for the experience with a particular person, you have cleared that Review Before Return choice for Soul Development.

Keep in mind, it is not your responsibility to adjust the energy of the person in question. You are responsible only for your Soul Development, and no one else's! If that person does not want to have an ongoing positive relationship with you, that is their Freewill choice to which you must adhere.

The illusion (misunderstanding) of Soul-Self Responsibility in healing the discord in your personal relationships, whether among family or friends, can be clarified by remembering that healing is a BI-liable experience. In other words, once you have given thanks for the experience, asked for wisdom to learn and grow, and attempted to make amends, you are cleared of further participation.

11

SENSATIONS
OF SILENCE

C onscious reasoning, taunted and antagonized by speculation, becomes a frantic effort when change has the potential to affect our job, living environment, personal relationships, investments, or any other facet of our daily lives. Yet, when our search for answers to anticipated changes is only through the conscious mind, it like running out into an unfamiliar darkness, desperately flailing our arms as we look for the solution.

Such behavior can also lead to many long and often meaningless conversations with family and friends, about the potential changes. It is true we have been conditioned to talk with our families, our priest, rabbi, minister or our friends when we anticipate change. However, from a Spiritual perspective, it is important to examine the inherent consequences of such an approach. While in human form, from a conscious perspective, our power to actuate change begins with our Thoughts, supported by our Words and set in motion by our Deeds. Our Freewill is the spark that ignites this power. Each Thought, each Word and each Action represents an energy that we set in motion, which then resonates throughout our Universe.

Thought, Word and Action energies are set in motion continually by every human, on a daily basis. These energies, projected from, and also through, the vessel of the human form, can be positive as well as negative. It is the non-discriminating qualities of these energies that must be considered in association with our Soul Development.

Solicitously examining the recesses of our family's and friends' opinions, thoughts and suggestions can produce a perpetual chaos within our own pathway (life). Conscious supplication of input from family or friends about change in our lives is tantamount to asking for the obstructive energy of judgment.

Consider. It is not unusual for people to say, categorically and unquestionably, that they trust their family and friends. However, we forget that these people are still in human form! While we may readily admit that our mother, father, sister, brother or friend is a worrier, a pessimist, and, in general a fear-based person, we eagerly seek their approbation for our plans. Frantically scurrying around, we hold up our plans for the worrier, the pessimist and the fear-based person to evaluate and endorse.

WHAT HAPPENS WHEN WE SEEK FAMILY'S AND FRIENDS' ADVICE

After you have spilled your guts about the potential changes in your life, these same people will talk to those they trust when you are not around. Their thoughts will also be focused on the conversations you have shared with them about the potential changes. While you may not hear the words they speak or know the thoughts they hold in their conscious minds, the energy of their opinions and fears will impact you nevertheless.

Furthermore, they might not comprehend the need or the reasons you feel you must make a change. Family members usually respond with remarks about love and wanting the best for us. However, consciously their only reference point is their past experience, whether similar or dissimilar to yours.

Friends often encourage friends to make change based on what they perceive that the person contemplating the change really wants. Family members as well as friends will of course use their own logic in determining what they would encourage in respect to your change. All such input is usually from a conscious prejudice, rather than from a Spiritual response.

These energies will accumulate in your pathway (life) as stumbling blocks of depression, sadness, doubts, fears, anxiety, lack of self-confidence, and so on. By way of comparison, let's consider how the vibration around our lives is influenced when we think of someone for a few days, the phone rings and it is them. The vibration has been influenced to perceive a thought process before an action (the phone call) is set in motion.

Moreover, our innate ability to perceive thought or word energy is not limited to phone calls. So, doesn't it stand to reason that if we can perceive a thought process in association with a phone call that is yet to be made, we will also be influenced by the thoughts as well as the words of those with whom we have been so anxious to consult?

A continuous resonance of thought, word and action energies, external as well as internal, influences our lives on a daily basis. Accordingly, unless you are seeking the help of a professional, it is far better consciously to keep silent and go within.

Keep in mind, it is not the change (challenge) that is

important; it is our response to the challenge (change) that provides the foundation for our Soul Development.

TRUSTING OUR FREEWILL

Allowing your Soul Mind to guide you will serve in keeping your pathway (life) clutter-free of the depression, sadness, doubt, fear, anxiousness, or lack of self confidence types of energies. In addition, this approach will assist in cutting the Blame-Thread that you would otherwise attach to the input from your family or friends.

Repeatedly in this writing I have pointed out the limitations of the conscious mind as it pertains to what it has learned or been taught in any given life. Our Soul Mind, our Spirit Mind (whatever label you choose is subjectively right), is unlimited.

It is the power of our Thoughts, Words and Deeds in the human experience that is fundamental in preparing our vibration for change. Therefore, it is crucial in our Soul Development that we use our Freewill to monitor our Thoughts, Words and Deeds on a continual basis.

When we choose to incorporate the energies of those we know, family as well as friends, into the symbolic representation of our potential changes, pollution is likely to occur. *In essence we are saying show me your fears, send me your doubts or, lend me your lack of self-confidence.*

SEEKING ADVICE FROM GOD

Prayer and meditation are the illuminators, providing the radiance that is more than sufficient to guide you along your Soul Path in any given life experience. Prayer alone is not enough to guide our lives in keeping with our Soul Contracts. Prayer is talking to God, while Meditation is the act of listening to God. Bear in mind however, that Meditation cannot occur in human form until you are willing. Freewill is key to the approach that sets aside your five senses from the conscious or external use. It is only through the five senses that the Soul Mind can, and most assuredly will, communicate with you.

The very moment you, by your Freewill approach, take hold of your breathing and begin to alter it, you send an automatic message to your Soul Mind that you want to communicate. Simply put, you are beginning to act like you want to listen to God. Our breathing is usually controlled by the Soul Mind along with the Subconscious Mind. Breathing deeply in through our nostrils and exhaling slowing through our mouth, interrupts this subtle control, notifying our Soul that we want to communicate.

Note: An easy way to remember the five senses: two T's, twoS's and one H. Taste, touch, see, smell and hear. These are the energies that the Spirit uses to communicate with the human form.

Should you seek the advice from a professional counselor, it is crucial to your Soul Development that you only consult with those who routinely pray and Meditate. If you choose to consult with a psychologist, psychiatrist or psychic, make sure that you inquire about the person's point of view concerning prayer and Meditation. If prayer and Meditation are not customary to their efforts, you are subject to a conscious bias, void of Spiritual insight.

Many times individuals seeking my counsel will say that I have confirmed what they already knew at a gut level. In reality they are telling me that their Spirit had previously given them the answer. I have merely provided the confirmation they needed at the time.

It is not unusual for individuals to seek corroboration for their plans from time to time. A well-known actor seeking my guidance before acceptance of a particular role was overjoyed when I encouraged him to take the part because it would be the vehicle for his comeback. (Which, by the way, it was!) You see, he had received that same message one day while sitting quietly in a meditative state. I had simply confirmed his own connection with the Spirit. "When two or more agree on any one thing. . . . "

Your Inner Voice, that Soul that is part of you each and every day, will guide you with an understanding and knowing that the conscious mind cannot comprehend without Prayer and Meditation. You will know that you know! We are mental, physical and Spiritual, all three in one!

In silence we can be shown and led in the way that is exalted for our Soul Development. The mysteries of the universe will become as common knowledge as we learn to commune with our Soul.

Other than a conscious knowledge of a potential change, we may also feel an impending change for which consciously we do not know the details. These types of feelings can infuse our energy field with such apprehension, uncertainty, and confusion that our conscious focus can become one of fear and dread. Whether the changes that have the potential of affecting our lives are known or felt, we can find the answer by going within.

Until we learn to wait on God in a Prayerful Meditative approach, we cannot know peace in relationship to change. In our silence, the Spirit will come to shine a light of guidance upon our pathway.

12

GREATNESS OF GRATITUDE

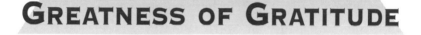

In the human experience, we all have those days when we think we cannot put one foot in front of the other. Life seems to be closing in on us from all sides. We cannot see how we can ever be free of the terror that has gripped our minds, let alone the difficulties that seem to be overflowing into our lives.

The waves of fear come crashing into our very being, like the waves generated by a hurricane that ravage the shoreline of coastal cities. Feelings of hopelessness and despair sneer at us with the expression of each thought. Every heartbeat seems to reverberate and magnify our desolation. Sinking lower and lower with each breath, we punish ourselves for not knowing how to abolish the destruction plaguing our lives.

Gloom struts ceremoniously at the head of the parade of depression circling our lives. Failure screams for attention, while jockeying for prominence in the fray. Our conscious mind has become the enemy in the camp, fighting to squeeze our very existence into a space of nothingness.

These fear-based illusions, generated by the conscious mind, devour our ability to move beyond the perpetual focus on the very antithesis of Faith: Fear!

When fear rather than Faith becomes our focus, our life begins to spin out of control, crashing into all of the demons that our conscious minds have been manipulating into our lives. The results of this type of focus resonate with the meaning of the old proverb that like begets like! So, too, with the maxim that what we fear we attract.

If only we would stop and realize that giving thanks for the opposition, asking for wisdom to learn and grow from it, sets in motion a healing force that releases our vibration from control by emotion! It is only through our efforts to connect with our Soul Mind or Spirit (whatever label you choose is subjectively right) that we will know the way of our Soul Path.

When we whine, moan, and groan about what we perceive as opposition, we heal nothing! We add to what we perceived as negative, turning further from any possibility of a positive outcome. Gratitude means acknowledgment—acknowledgment that the opposition is a Soul Growth Issue or a Soul Grief Choice. Chosen during The Review Before Return Process, we must remember that our Soul Development will be greatly enhanced by our association with these choices.

A SPIRITUAL JOURNEY

During the mid-eighties, when the chapter titles of this book were given to me in a vision, I began a portion of my life's journey that would forever change who I was and who I would become.

The journey I set out on at that juncture of my life would forever impress upon me how limited our conscious minds are in terms of the bigger picture of our human, earth-life experience. I had been working several years as a professional accountant, during which time I was not following my Spiritual Path. I had known since my childhood that I wanted to somehow help people in need. However, I had refused to use my psychic gifts to assist anyone from the mid-seventies until the mid-eighties, about a ten-year period.

At the time, I lived in Texas, along with most every other person in the state; I was affected by the downturn in the oil economy. I had worked for several years as secretary-treasurer/controller at a shipyard. We built not only ships, but most of the semi-submersible oil rigs in the Gulf of Mexico.

As the downward-spiraling economy tightened its grip on the state, the company went from a roster of several thousand employees to a roster of around three hundred within a very short span of months.

A little over a year after the process began, the company was down to a few key employees. After the company was sold, some of the key employees were sent to our sister company in Pennsylvania. Those of us who were left tightened our belts, dug in our heels, and determined not to give up.

After all, how could a company that had been in business for more than 117 years, had employed thousands of people, and was recognized world wide go out of business? Something had to happen.

Well, something did happen. About a year after being sold, the company went into Chapter 11, Reorganization Bankruptcy.

It took another year before the last breath was drawn. Try as we might, the company would disappear from the face of the earth.

The president of the company and a handful of people struggled to eke out a living doing barge repair. The once-renowned company would build no more ships nor jack up oil rigs. The handful of people who started the barge repair facility remained in Orange, Texas, while the rest of us tried to collect what was left of our lives and move into our future.

I managed to find a job as controller of an office machine dealership. It took everything I could muster to tolerate the tyrannical environment in which the owner was accustomed to working. Not only had I taken a drastic cut in salary, I was now working for a person who treated everyone like children. He and I often locked horns.

I could no longer subject myself to a person whose modus operandi was management by intimidation. The man was brilliant in the marketing arena. Administratively, however, his interpersonal skills were noteworthy only by their absence.

After two years of struggling to keep my sanity while denying my self-respect, I decided to quit and open my own business. I wanted to open a storefront selling radios, televisions, office machinery and equipment, and anything else that was legal. I would also offer shipping, office supplies, fax capabilities, mail boxes, notary service and copying service. I begin to look around for a location I could afford.

As it turned, out a friend of mine had leased an office building in a small town between the town where I lived and the town where I used to work in the shipyard. She offered me space in her building at such a reasonable rate, that I felt that I should take advantage of the offer.

DOWN THE WRONG ROAD

Everyone in the tri-state area knew that the town of which I speak was notorious for their uncompromising prejudice against minorities, particularly African-Americans. Why I would even consider going into a town like this could only have to do with my self-imposed desperation. However, it would take two more years of agony before the reality of such thinking would affect my life.

I was so desperate in my thinking at the time that I chose to ignore the fact that this town was a hotbed of prejudice and hate. Even though I grew up in the South, I had never embraced prejudice. The only hate that I had ever personally felt was reserved for certain family members.

Using my psychic gifts to make my way in life was not even a consideration at the time. I had put that aside nearly ten years before. Anyway, the area where I lived at the time was very judgmental about that sort of thing. It was part of the Bible Belt, where people were more fanatical in their beliefs than most. Desperate in my thinking, I set out into this darkness, flailing my arms about, trying to find my way.

Determined to keep my house, I was eager to find the formula by which this could be accomplished. I was totally focused through the conscious perspective. Any supplication to God was filled with a sense of anger and abandonment.

One day, feeling particularly vulnerable and hopeless, I stood at the French doors of my dining room that overlooked my back yard, looked up into the sky and began to yell at God. "If you want me to sit in sackcloth and ashes, tell me and I will build the damn fire!"

Immediately, my mind flashed on the parable of Job. According to Biblical scripture, Job had lost everything and was encouraged to curse God and die. I was so incensed by this memory that I hit the wall with my fist and yelled, "F__Job! I don't intend on losing a damn thing!" I would learn later on how much I would gain, rather than lose from this whole life-changing experience.

However, as the days slowly passed, I would find myself thinking as I walked through my home, *I don't need a formal dining room. I don't need a formal living room.* With this type of focus it wasn't long before I had mentally reduced my home to no more than a warehouse, used to house possessions that I really did not need.

TRAVELING WITH EYES CLOSED

Having reduced my life to one of whining, moaning and groaning, I chose not to be consciously aware that it was my behavior that was continuing to attract more turmoil into my life. I had forgotten the answer was not external, but within. I had known this in my past, but I had become so immersed in my fear-based thinking that my Soul Mind was shut out altogether.

The store I opened occupied a space that was only 8 feet by 12 feet. Also, I had never sold anything in my entire life. I had always worked as an accountant. Looking back, I can not explain why I consciously thought I could shift from a known profession of accounting to retail sales. Yet in retrospect there were so many road signs along the way, I should have realized that a Higher Power than my conscious mind was at work in my life. *For that I have expressed Gratitude.*

HARD TRAVELING

For five months, I never left the confines of this 8-by-12 space. Each day I would spend most of the day calling potential customers on the phone. To my amazement, it worked. In the five months that I had that business, I set records for sales in the area without ever personally meeting any of my customers. In fact, an individual who owned a similar business was so upset by my success he called and threatened my life. He said he could not be responsible for what might happen to me. He also said I was stealing his business. I was not. I was simply selling office machinery and equipment at just a few hundred dollars over cost.

Most of the people in the business at the time were accustomed to charging their customers double or triple of wholesale. Their overhead included expensive storefront facilities plus a large amount of in-stock merchandise. My approach was just the opposite. I did not keep merchandise in stock, nor was my overhead high.

About that time, a friend of mine who lived in Delaware invited me to come and visit him. He lived in a corporate condo and told me that staying with him would cost nothing. He said I should consider coming for a few days and looking around for a better opportunity. Texas was still reeling from the economic downturn suffered from the oil recession. With no improvement in sight, I accepted his offer. And, although I was setting records for sales in the area, my profit margin was not sufficient for financial survival. In the five months that I had been in business, I had managed to sell almost a half a million dollars worth of office machinery and equipment.

Hospitals, schools, businesses and individuals alike were scrambling to buy from me. I was only charging a hundred or two over cost. Incredibly, I had managed to do this all by myself and on the phone. Yet I was barely making enough profit to pay the rent on my office space, my mortgage, car payment and food and gas.

Without realizing it, I had positioned myself in such a way that I would learn to receive instead of always giving. Up until that time in my life, I had always been the doer and the giver. I was the one that helped others. Now suddenly I was in a position where I had nothing to give, but rather had much that I needed. I was on the verge of losing my home, and my car needed $1,060 in repairs. I did not know from week to week if I would make enough sales to sustain my life.

However, the value of this struggle cannot be measured in terms of a dollar sign. I was truly allowed to see how God will send angels to lift us up so that we do not stumble against the rocks. It took such an experience in my life for me to reconnect with my Inner Spirit. *For this I have Gratitude.*

A TURNING POINT

One day a lady with whom I had worked for years in the shipyard called and asked me how I was doing. She happened to call me on a day when the despair in my life was so intense that I did not feel there was any way out.

I was more than two months behind on my mortgage payment. That morning I had received a call from the purchasing agent of a local hospital telling me that a very large order had been put on indefinite hold. I desperately needed that sale to catch up my mortgage. After listening to my story, my dear friend told me not to worry—that she just knew things would work out for me.

Later that afternoon this same dear friend stopped by my business for a visit. I felt so elated that she would take the time to drive twenty-five miles to come and visit me, particularly knowing the despair I was feeling after our phone conversation earlier that day.

She and I talked for several minutes until my phone rang and someone wanted an immediate quote on two high-end fax machines. I was so anxious to get off the phone and visit further with my friend that I hurriedly quoted the person an amount that underbid my competitors by less than ten dollars. I would come to realize in just a little over a week that this potential order seemed surely to have been orchestrated by a Higher Power.

It took me several minutes to complete the phone call and when I finally hung up my friend said she had to run several more errands and should be going. As she prepared to leave she put what I thought was a card of encouragement on the counter.

The phone rang again. I answered, put the person on hold, hugged my friend, and thanked her for the visit. As she left I went back to the phone call. The individual wanted me to fax a quote on several copy machines and typewriters. It took more than two hours to do the research, prepare the quote and fax it.

After completing the task, I again noticed the card that my friend had left for me. When I opened the card, I could not believe my eyes. There was $3,500 in cash inside the envelope, with a brief note. The note said that she hoped this would help me and not to worry about repayment.

The note went on to say that I was to give it back when I could, no hurry. I burst out in tears. I had no idea that she had come to see me for this reason. I also did not know that it would take nearly two years before I could repay her.

My phone rang again. This time it was my friend in Delaware inquiring as to when I wanted to come up and look around. I told him I could not afford to go. There was the matter of travel. I could not drive my car. It needed more than a thousand dollars worth of work. My friend told me he had more than enough frequent flyer mileage from his travels to send me a ticket.

I was reluctant to accept help from yet another friend. However, my friend insisted, and we finally agreed on a day and time. I was to make arrangements to go that coming weekend. Since it was Tuesday, I did not have much time to contemplate the trip. If I had, I would not have gone. So, I made my plans accordingly.

I loved Delaware. What beauty! Not only did the rolling hills, beautiful trees and fabulous houses appeal to me, my friend told me I could live in the corporate condo for free as long as I needed. I decided to return to Texas, lease my house, close my business and make the move.

With excitement, I left Delaware to return to Texas. It was the first time in many months that I had allowed myself to believe that something positive was happening.

More Angels along the Way

All the way back on the plane I prayed and meditated. It had taken all of the turmoil of the last few months for me to finally let go and let God take over. I asked God to give me a sign that the move was indeed the thing I should do. The moment I returned home, more miracles began to unfold.

When I arrived home that evening there was a message on my answering machine from a friend who wanted to talk to me. It was so late I decided that I would call her the next day from my work.

The next morning when I went to my store, the lady who owned the building came running out to my car. She told me that the person to whom I had given the quote for the two fax machines wanted to place the order immediately. He had been trying to reach me for three days! The profit I made on those two machines was within five dollars of the amount I needed to do the repair on my car! There was my sign!
For that I had Gratitude.

I was so excited I forgot to return the call that my friend had left on my answering machine the previous day. However, when I got home that evening she had left another message.

A co-worker's house had burned down and the woman lost everything.

Since I had mentioned a few weeks earlier that I might move to Delaware, she wanted to know if I had anything to sell. I had told her that if I moved to Delaware I would have to get rid of a lot of stuff. The condo my friend had offered was about half as big as my house, and I did not intend to put anything in storage.

Without having to turn a hand, everything that I needed to dispose of was sold! This same friend also said she wanted to get together soon. We made plans for lunch that weekend. My friend was aware that I had been struggling. I was trying to sell enough office equipment to pay my bills and to pay for the U-Haul that I was going to rent for the move.

During lunch, my friend gave me a check for $1,500 and said she hoped that would help. I could not believe that another friend was offering me exactly what I needed at the time. She, too, implored me not to worry about repayment. She said she felt it was in Divine order that she assist me. It would also take me almost two years to repay her this amount.

A NEW TURN IN THE PATH

For most of my life, with the exception of the ten-year respite in Texas, I have been doing psychic work, counseling people individually as well as working with the legal authorities. During my stay in Delaware, I decided to do my counseling again, at least until I found an accounting position. So, I found two radio stations that allowed me to do weekly shows, one in Wilmington and one in Dover. Meanwhile, I sent out more than 700 résumés trying to obtain a position in accounting, with no luck.

The competition for jobs at the vice president of finance or controller level is very keen. In that place and time, it was an employer's market. In retrospect, I believe a Higher Power was again at work in my life.

After I had done two shows a week for more than a year, an article appeared in a national radio and television magazine about my work. I had no idea that getting back into the psychic work would take me to Phoenix, Arizona, in less than two years of my move to Delaware.

A station from Arizona had me on as a guest. The success was so great, the producers wanted me back again and again. Some wonderful people who now live in Colorado on their ranch flew me out to Arizona after hearing me several times on the radio. *For this I have Gratitude.*

My friends graciously opened their home to me, set me up to see clients, and insisted that I consider relocating to Arizona. I would stay with these wonderful people for almost six months before making the decision to buy a home here. Living in a desert did not appeal to me at all. I had always lived around, water, grass and trees. Never having lived in a desert before, I was very anxious about the heat.

However, I was so busy in Arizona that I hardly had time to think. After being with my friends in Arizona for about four months, I received a call from some friends and clients in Houston, Texas. They wanted me to come there in about six weeks and do a couple of seminars. They would also arrange for me to do two radio shows as well as a television show.

OFF THE TRACK AGAIN

Man, was I excited! I was going back to where there was water, trees and grass! Six weeks later, I loaded my computer, clothes and everything that I had brought to Arizona in my car and headed back to Texas. If I was to do psychic work, at least I would be in a place that I liked!

I did not once stop to think that the Spirit had led me to Arizona. In retrospect, I now believe that indeed the Spirit led me to Arizona to complete this book and, to return again to my Soul Path, helping people with my psychic gifts.

In Houston, I had been invited to stay with a client who owned a very large house in River Oaks. She insisted that she considered it a privilege for me to stay with her and her son. I arrived a day earlier than initially planned and wanted to spend the day visiting with other friends whom I had not seen in a couple of years.

Since my client was not expecting me until a day later, I decided to stay in a hotel the night I arrived in Houston. The next morning when I was preparing to leave, I looked out of my window and noticed something all over the hood of my car. When I went outside to see what it was, I was infuriated to find that someone had apparently gotten very drunk and thrown up all over my car from the balcony just above my room.

That was just the beginning. My stay in Houston went downhill from that point. The two seminars that I was to conduct were canceled. The people who were making the arrangements were thrown out of the facility for non-payment of rent. The radio shows that I was to do bumped me to cover a hot political issue going on at the time. The television show was canceled because the woman who was to interview me suddenly moved out of state.

The client with whom I was staying in Houston had arranged for me to have session with her, many of her relatives, and some friends while I was there. This kept me busy for several days.

About a week after my arrival in Texas, I called my friends in Arizona and asked them if I could come back. They were excited that things did not work out in Houston. They were delighted that I had come to my senses and wanted to come back where they felt I belonged. *For these friends, I have Gratitude!*

I left the next morning around four in the morning for my return trip to Arizona. I drove straight through. It took me 18 hours and 40 minutes. When I pulled up in their driveway around 10:30 p.m. they ran out embraced me and took me back into their home. They were certain, even though I did not know at the time, that I was supposed to be in Arizona!

THE RIGHT DESTINATION

I am now in my eleventh year of living in Arizona and can say that these people are still some of my most cherished friends. Even though they abandoned me and moved to Colorado, I love them dearly. They have a beautiful ranch in Bayfield, Colorado, with a five-bedroom guest house. I try to make a trip to their place at least once a year.

I have Gratitude for all the oppositions that I have known. I know without a shadow of a doubt, these experiences have served as parameters for my Soul Path. The twenty-five years of my accounting profession fade into obscurity when held up against the backdrop of my Soul Contract.

For this I have Gratitude.

I have Gratitude for those who have helped me along the way. These people I believe were Angels in my Pathway, sent to assist and encourage me in choosing the Pathway of my Soul Contract!

Beth and Bill of *The Beth and Bill Radio Show,* KEZ 99.9, have also been Angels in my Path. For nine-plus years, once each month, I have been a guest on their show. During that time we have laughed together and cried

Beth, Fred & Bill

together. and I am thankful to say, continue to offer hope and Spiritual help to their listeners. For ten years their show has been number one in the charts. I feel truly blessed to have been a small part of such a wonderfully progressive show! Beth and Bill to me are Angels of the radio waves!

I have experienced an energy in the desert that I have not known in any other place. The energy seems to be a very base vibration that nurtures a new start. Over the years, it has been my personal experience to witness many people who have come to the desert to separate themselves from all that they have known, while Spiritually renewing their lives. *For this I have Gratitude!*

What can I say about Fred Rawlins that he doesn't already know I'm going to say about him? Fred has been an entertaining, interesting, and popular guest on our morning radio shoe for many years. Fred not only has the ability to make people laugh and to laugh at himself, but he also pushes them to perform introspection and self examination. He's a psychic who teaches us to examine our psyche and learn to trust our instincts. In other words, what Fred tells you is many times something you already knew but didn't want to know how to face. I get the feeling that Fred isn't afraid to say, "See, you didn't really need to ask me. just trust your gut." And that's why we love him.

–Beth McDonald
The Beth and Bill Show, KEZ Radio FM 99.9

Fred is one of my favorite guests on our little nickel-and-dime radio show. Just about the time you think he is making something up, he will really connect with the caller he is doing a mini-reading for. He can really nail the readings. Plus he has a great sense of humor. We don't call him "Our Surly Psychic" without reason. Fred has done personal readings for me over the last decade, and with most of the time, right after he has done it you think, "Well I just don't get that." But sure enough within a span of time, well it's just amazing how accurate he ends up being. OK it's a little spooky too. But don't ever forget that underneath all the glitzy showbiz exterior, Fred is a really decent, caring, spiritual, and most of all, loving human. It does not get much better than that.

–Bill Austin
The Beth and Bill Show, KEZ Radio FM 99.9

One Hundred Spiritual Equations
and Maxims

1. Guilt = Dependence.
   Guilt implies consciously as well as subconsciously that someone has an answer that you do not have.
2. Self Judgment = Discord to Our Spirit.
   Self-judgment occurs when we rebuke ourselves for the past. We must embrace the past in order to grow Self-judgment also occurs when we condemn others for what they have done. We are all connected to the Universal Subconsciousness. Therefore, when we judge (condemn) others', we judge (condemn) our selves. Self-judgment knows no equal in the uni verse.
3. Spirituality = Caring about Others.
   This requires the unlearning of Self-Judgment.
4. Emotions = Conscious Response.
   If we allow emotions to precede our actions or changes, we will run amok! Emotions are offensive to our Spirit for Soul Development.
5. Recognition = Soul Growth Issue.
   We cannot be emotional about something with which we are not familiar. Once you recognize the meaning of an issue, it can no longer control you.
6. Origin = Destiny.
   Spiritually, we are trying to return to that God Force of pure Love, from whence all Souls "Origin-ated."
7. Conscious Mind = Limited.
   Consciousness is limited to what you have learned or been taught in any given life. The Conscious Mind cannot perceive a future; it is a historical database.

Looking to the future the Conscious Mind would perceive what is ahead as a fear of the unknown.

8. Soul Mind = Unlimited.

This source of Knowledge is a reservoir which contains information relevant to the Past, Present and Future in terms of our Soul Development.

9. Denial of Past Actions = Impediment to healing.

Denial prevents any attempt to heal. As long as responsibility for our actions is denied, there is no basis for healing to begin.

10. Conscious Living requires a defensive covering or armor. This armor is constructed with excuses, blaming others, fear and emotions. Spiritual Living requires only Faith.

11. Living Spiritually = How We Treat One Another determines our Spirituality.

All else is theory.

12. Misnomer = "The" truth.

A misnomer often occurs in the human experience when individualized beliefs are called "the" truth.

13. Freewill = The Spark That Ignites.

Freewill ignites the power of our thoughts, words and deeds.

14. Wisdom, from a Spiritual perspective, is a cumulative (life after life) harmonizing energy, culminating in pure LOVE.

15. Like = A Conscious Expression. Love = A Spiritual Expression.

If you dislike someone (family or friend), you are not required to be around them. You are required however, to love them Spiritually.

16. Other people's judgments do not have to be your compass in life.

17. Truth = Your Truth. Truth is Spiritually *subjective.*

18. Our most difficult challenges (Soul Growth Issues) usually occur in our childhood. It is usually the only time that we are totally dependent on someone else.

19. Past = Experience!

The past is not a way of life unless you make it so.

20. To decry the past or present challenges only adds to the pain we have already endured, exaggerating the "time spent" requirement for that particular Soul Growth Issue.

21. Your life will chase after your thoughts. Your thoughts will not chase you down the street.

22. Appraise the "value" of the challenge.

Ask yourself if you are willing to trade your future, which is unlimited, for such a paltry sum?

23. Do not linger around the past. It is an emotionally spent energy.

24. Our past consists of experiences (lessons) in which we reacted emotionally rather than Spiritually.

25. Until you have walked in the other person's shoes, your knowledge remains Conscious, NOT Spiritual.

26. A Soul Grief Choice provides the mechanism by which God's Love will be demonstrated in an earthly environment.

27. Soul-Self Responsibility is principal for our Soul Development endeavors.

28. You will add to others' sorrow if you speak with a voice of judgment and condemnation.

29. Nothing that separates, segregates or sets itself apart can be of God.

30. Nothing that takes away Freewill can be of God.

31. Inactivity starves the Spirit.

While it is good to think positive and speak that way, Faith without works is dead. We must take action.

32. Illusions = Other's Opinions

This is true even when we seek their advice.

33. "You will notice in all disputes between Christians since the birth of the Church, Rome has always favored the doctrine which most completely subju gated the human mind and annihilated reason."

—Voltaire

34. Perfection cannot exist in the human form.

35. The investment we make to meditate each day, ten to fifteen minutes, provides a payback that is astronomical! Spending one percent of our time during a twenty-four-hour period to meditate is so powerful that it serves to heal the other 99% of our lives.

36. The more emotional an issue is, the more acceptable it seems to be to the conscious mind.

37. Freewill by its very expression will abolish others' control over us.

38. Co-Dependence = Emotional Control.

People connected to our lives cannot build their own foundation as long as we continue to take their tools.

39. Giving thanks for a challenge (experience) disallows the experience from controlling you emotionally.

40. Giving thanks for a challenge (experience) disallows the experience from being repetitive in your life.

41. Giving thanks for a challenge (experience) will con nect the conscious thought to the Spiritual Mind, allowing you to understand the benefit from the experience, in relationship to your Soul Development.

42. Like begets like. We must use our Freewill to monitor our Thoughts, our Words, and our Actions each day. We have a responsibility for our future as well as to our Souls to insure that these three areas are positive.

43. Our future rests on the foundation of our Thoughts, our Words, and our Deeds.

44. Our future can be better than our attitude, but we have to change it first.

45. The only thing between you and your future is an attitude.

46. Do not try to make plans for your future while using excuses from your past.

47. We must learn to observe life without letting the emotions of the event control or possess us.

48. If we are walking in Faith, it means that we do not take our burdens with us.

49. Judgment is often cloaked as advice.

50. Within our Spirit Mind or Higher Selves, there is a plan that is perfect for our life in relationship to our Soul Development.

51. There is loftiness in God's way. Through it, we can be lifted above the trials of life.

52. Emotional expectations that do not occur bring about fear.

53. When we discourage people from making changes, we discourage the possibility of opportunities from being experienced.

54. Out of aggravation judgment is often born.

55. Faith means going forward with your life without all of the answers given at once, or without a blueprint put into your hand.

56. Giving too much to another diminishes the recipient's concept of self-achievement.

57. When we sit by the wayside of life allowing ourenergy to spill out around what we have perceived to be a loss, it reduces our future to no more than our fear.

58. You have a choice to make each day. Will you con
tinue to live your challenges, or will you continue
with your life?

59. Get your head out of your IF'S! Avoiding the If-
Onlies loop is a must for Spiritual Development.

60. Focusing continually on the imaginary details of
what may happen, summons the fear you are
focused on into your life. Do not set the stage for a
play before you have the script!

61. The bigger the challenge, the more forgiveness we
need to impart.

62. The more balanced we become Spiritually, the more
challenges will deflect from us.

63. We should not earmark our blessings. That is an
indication of a lack of Faith. Many of us have to
learn to give ourselves permission to have abun
dance. We have allowed the "patterned responses"
from our formative years to rule our lives.

64. There is no distance between you and your future.
There is only an attitude.

65. The Vision of your future cannot be constructed
with the memories of your past.

66. Physically and mentally we can draw on the Soul
Reserves derived from our efforts to meditate. This
will sustain us throughout our day.

67. The family that we choose helps to keep the
parameters around our Spiritual Contract.

68. If we clear the energy with someone, we are not
required to reincarnate with that Soul in
subsequent lives.

69. Complex challenges (experiences) during the human
sojourn do not depict the judgment of a vengeful
God being ruthlessly inflicted on an unloved Soul.

70. The more emotional something is, the more believable it seems to be to the conscious mind.

71. There is no such thing as an unloved Soul in the Spirit realm. Therefore, labels such as illegitimate, minority, poor, homeless, sick, disadvantaged, uneducated, and the like are not applicable in the Spirit Realm.

72. Illusions of Sameness often become embedded in our conscious minds to such a degree that change cannot occur.

73. The human experience is the only time the Soul is instantaneously influenced by Freewill.

74. Change is often the mechanism that eradicates illusions.

75. Past Lives experiences are reflected into our future as Soul Growth Issues (illusions) from our past, expressed through contact with the patterns of energy into which we reincarnate.

76. While in human form, our power to actuate change begins with our Thoughts, supported by our Words and set in motion by our Deeds.

77. Input from family and friends is usually from a con scious prejudice, rather than from a Spiritual response.

78. When we choose to incorporate the energies of those we know, family as well as friends, into the symbolic representation of our potential changes, pollution is likely to occur. In essence we are saying, show me your fears, send me your doubts, or lend me your lack of self-confidence.

79. Meditation is the ACT of listening to God. Meditation is God talking to YOU!

80. It is only through the five senses that the Soul Mind can, and most assuredly will, communicate with you.

81. If Prayer and Meditation are not customary to the efforts of those you seek with whom to confer, you are subjecting yourself to a conscious bias, void of Spiritual insight.

82. *Until we learn to wait on God in a Prayerful Meditative approach, we cannot know peace in relationship to change. In our silence, the Spirit will come to shine a light of guidance, illuminating the pathway to follow that is in keeping with our Soul Contract.*

83. Many times the indoctrination that is endured in our formative years leaves an acrimonious imprint in our vibrations; a bitter taste.

84. The patterns of energy on which an individual imprinted during the formative years can harass the adult life until a conscious effort is made to redefine the vibration.

85. Quite often during a particularly stressful period, we will mimic the behavior patterns that we were exposed to and imprinted on during our formative years.

86. In a knee-jerk response, we will exhibit energy patterns just like those expressed by our parents.

87. If our parents were prone to making us feel guilty in our childhood, it was an experience our Soul chose during The Review Before Return Process.

88. Hate is presented in as well as through our belief systems.

89. When emotions and stress collide in our lives, flashbacks of behavior patterns can come spilling out of our energy, causing a repetition of our Soul Growth Issues.

90. By harboring hate for anything or anyone, we make provisions for a negative response.

91. Suppressing imprints of behavior patterns from our formative years will deny healing and advancement in our Soul Development.

92. We must embrace and give thanks for all of the misery we have known if we are to have healing IN our Souls.

93. Soul Growth Issues as well as Soul Grief Choices are not always monumental in their scope.

94. The thought energy you devote to whining, moaning and groaning will rehabilitate, restoring to its former state, the challenge (experience) in your vibration.

95. Consciously assessing the plight of someone in need does not make known the individual's Soul Growth Issues or Soul Grief Choices to the observer.

96. The human psyche usually must crash impetuously into a few trials and tribulations before the effort of listening is accomplished.

97. Rushing in to apply compassion to another person's life without a Prayerful Meditative Approach is akin to playing Russian roulette with both Souls.

98. Codependency causes our efforts to be transformed from a gift out of our hand to a debt for our Soul.

99. Freewill seems to demand several years of experience to be used with confidence.

100. Ego is the conscious byproduct of the beliefs that we chose to experience during our Review Before Return Process.

MIRACLE JOURNAL

As you begin the process of developing and keeping your own personal Miracle Journal, you must reflect on the past as well as the present. This contemplation should be approached from a Spiritual point of view. Reflection on preceding or current circumstances without the Spiritual response serves only to increase the time spent with each Soul Growth Issue.

With each challenge (experience), we have an opportunity to learn, gain insight and create Spiritual Growth by our response. If we respond emotionally with resentment or negativity, the challenge (experience) becomes repetitious. If we respond Spiritually—giving thanks and asking for wisdom to learn and grow—the challenge (experience) becomes an integral building block in the process of our Soul Development. What we consciously perceive as the stumbling block, when Spiritualized will take us one step further in the—completing of—our Soul Development.

EXAMPLE
DATE: JULY 22, 2002:
CONSCIOUS PERSPECTIVE: *Reflected on move to Delaware: Consciously this was a move that I felt initially was a new beginning. I was excited about doing two radio shows per week for my psychic work. However, I would find that this effort would only produce about 4 to 6 clients a month. Frustrated, I began to send out résumés in response to companies that were looking for an experienced controller or vice president of finance. After a year and a half, and seven hundred and three resumes, with minimal results, I felt I had to make a change. Disappointment loomed large in my thoughts each day. A friend*

suggested that I try and get an article in the Radio and Television Magazine, a national publication. I did. It was that article that brought me to Arizona. A radio station saw the article, called, and had me on the show by phone. The success was overwhelming. A couple who heard me on the program called me, scheduled a session with me, and subsequently called to say they wanted to fly me out to stay with them a few days. The radio show that I had done by phone was more than willing to have me on in person. I was on that show for two years before getting on the Beth and Bill Show, where I have been for 11+ years. The rest is history.

SPIRITUAL DISCERNMENT OF EVENT: *I had been whining and moaning about why the Spirit would have me move to Delaware when I left Texas rather than moving directly to Arizona. One night in a dream I was told to give thanks for the Delaware challenge (experience) and I would understand. A few weeks later it was revealed to me that there were several reasons the move had to occur in the order that it did. One of the key factors in the move to Arizona was the article in the National Radio and Television publication. The remaining dynamics of the Delaware move had to do with a Soul Grief Choice connected to a handful of people in that area. I had contracted Spiritually to assist these individuals in this lifetime. For that challenge (experience) I give thanks.*

ASSOCIATED MIRACULOUS OUTCOME: *The Soul Grief Choice I experienced in Delaware will be shared in detail in my next book. However, let me say that moving to Arizona helped to ground me in a way that I had not known in the past; I almost felt trapped at first. I know that I came to Arizona to reconnect Spiritually, finish this book and begin a work that would become the foundation for the work that I would continue for the duration of this life. For this I give thanks.*

A woe-is-me or poor-pitiful-me evaluation of our past or present is counterproductive to Spiritual Development. Healing can take place only when we embrace the past, or the present, give thanks for the challenge (experience) and ask for wisdom to learn and grow from it.

What we may consciously recognize as the stumbling block, once Spiritualized, becomes the stepping stone. So as you undertake to recount the tribulations of the past, or present, keep in mind that the development of a Miracle Journal will serve to illuminate the pathway that is in keeping with your Soul Contract; your future!

DATE: _____

CONSCIOUS PERSPECTIVE OF EVENT: _____

_____

_____

_____

_____

_____

_____

_____

_____

SPIRITUAL DISCERNMENT OF EVENT: _____

_____

_____

_____

_____

_____

_____

_____

_____

ASSOCIATED MIRACULOUS OUTCOME: _____

_____

_____

_____

_____

_____

_____

_____

_____

DATE: _____

CONSCIOUS PERSPECTIVE OF EVENT:

_____
_____
_____
_____
_____
_____
_____
_____

SPIRITUAL DISCERNMENT OF EVENT:

_____
_____
_____
_____
_____
_____
_____
_____

ASSOCIATED MIRACULOUS OUTCOME:

_____
_____
_____
_____
_____
_____
_____
_____

THE COMMANDMENTS	THE CALL
1. I am the LORD your God, you shall have no other gods before me.	Faith (Trust in God)
2. You shall not take the Name of the LORD your God in vain.	Respect, Holiness
3. Keep holy the Sabbath day.	Renewal
4. Honor your father and your mother.	Family
5. You shall not kill.	Respect for Life
6. You shall not commit adultery.	Chastity Faithfulness (Fidelity)
7. You shall not steal.	Justice (Honesty)
8. You shall not bear false witness.	Truth
9. You shall not covet your neighbor's wife	Purity
10. You shall not covet your neighbor's goods.	Generosity

THE TEN COMMANDMENTS

THE ACTION

All faith in God, freedom from Lesser gods: wealth, sex power, popularity.

Respect for God and the things of God: prayer worship

Not just the Sabbath rest but setting aside time for prayer, good recreation,quite reflection.

Loving care and respect for all family members, elders and younger siblings, too. Respect for elders in general.

Courtesy to all, speaking respectfully to all, seeking the best for all. Respecting others' freedom while defending all human life.

Faithful actions beyond just abstaining from sexual contact outside of marriage. Respect for sex and marriage.

Concern for the rights of others... A commitment fairness and a willingness to suffer loss rather than depriving another.

A dedication to what is real and true, even it that is against our interests.

A desire to want only what God wills. A single-hearted devotion to God's way.

A cooperation in God's own generosity that sees all goods as belonging to God and freely given for the good of all.

Copyright 2000 William E. Rushman

TESTIMONIALS

Fred Rawlins has been providing solid, meaningful counsel that has helped improve the lives of people all over the world for a long long time. Fred's personal journey of discovery is inspiring in its own right. Soul Growth Issues-Soul Grief Choices provides the tools of introspection that brings his special gifts of insight to everyone who reads this incredible book.

–Win Holden
Book and Magazine Publisher

Most of us stumble through life as if walking through an unfamiliar house in the dark, tripping over the unexpected obstacles the block our paths. Fred flips on the light switch in this compelling presentation of Soul Growth Issues-Soul Grief Choices.

–R. Frederick Linfesty, Esq.

Soul Growth Issues-Soul Grief Choices has provided me with a light in the tunnel of life. Fred's subtle wit and his ability to view glimpses into the future have been inspiring. As Fred has allowed me to see this book during its birth, I have realized that this book is for YOU, the reader. Experience a wondrous amazing journey as you learn how to be at one with your Divine Creator. Get ready to start living life and not just existing!

–C.Grande, President
Magney-Grande